Women,

Women, Power, and Subversion

JUDITH
LOWDER NEWTON

Power, and Subversion

SOCIAL STRATEGIES IN BRITISH FICTION, 1778–1860

THE UNIVERSITY OF GEORGIA PRESS
ATHENS

Athens, Georgia 30602

Designed by Sandra Strother
Set in 10 on 13 Trump Medieval type
PRINTED IN THE UNITED STATES OF AMERICA

Library of Congress Cataloging in Publication Data

Newton, Judith Lowder.
Women, power, and subversion.

Bibliography: p.
Includes index.
1. English fiction—Women authors—History and criticism. 2. Women in literature. 3. Power (Social sciences) in literature. 4. Feminism and literature. 5. English fiction—19th century—History and criticism. I. Title.
PR830.W62N4 823'.009'9287 81-1068
ISBN 0-8203-0564-2 AACR2

Portions of this book are based on the following previously published articles by Judith Newton: "*Pride and Prejudice:* Power, Fantasy and Subversion in Jane Austen," *Feminist Studies*, vol. 4, no. 1 (February 1978); and "*Evelina:* or, The History of a Young Lady's Entrance into the Marriage Market," *Modern Language Studies*, vol. 6, no. 1 (Spring 1976). The author and the publisher wish to thank Feminist Studies, Inc., and the Northeast Modern Language Association for permission to reprint the material here.

TO DICK

Contents

Acknowledgments

Writing, though often solitary, is not an isolated act. It is part of history—and not merely a history of ideas but a history of material conditions too. I could not have written this book without time to myself and money on which to live, and that I did write it is due first to the liberality of La Salle College, which gave me a year's leave with full pay. I am very thankful. I am also thankful to the American Council of Learned Societies for the grant-in-aid which made it possible to finish the project I had begun.

Writing this book has been part of a history which is the history of friendships as well. It is no longer clear to me, for example, at what point some of Rachel Blau DuPlessis' best ideas became my own. She read and reread this manuscript with a generosity, a carefulness, and a vision that I am very grateful for and that are a model to me of what feminist criticism and editing should be about. I am also very thankful to Nina Auerbach and Sandra Gilbert for their fine readings of this text and to Ros Petchesky, Mary Ryan, Judy Stacey, Judy Walkowitz, and Steve Zelnick for their helpful insights into specific sections.

I owe more to Uli Knoepflmacher than I can perhaps make clear. I am grateful to him not just for his reading of this manuscript but for his painstaking—and inspirational—direction of my dissertation, an act which first enabled me to write, and I am grateful for his continued support of me and my work, for his friendship, and for his letters (complete with *underscorings* and exclamation points!), which have cheered and strengthened me over the years.

I am also indebted to people who never read this manuscript but whose histories have shaped my own. I am thankful to Ed Foulks for the revitalizing and reconstructive work we did together, work that has permanently empowered me in my life. I am thankful to my colleagues Caryn McTighe Musil and Barbara Cassacci Millard for eight years of friendship, intellectual companionship, candlelight dinners, solidarity, and humor. And I am thankful to many of my students at La Salle College for our history of teaching and learning together.

Above all, however, I am grateful to Richard C. Newton, who read and reread this manuscript—and most of the other manuscripts I have written—with an insight, a generosity, and a tact which have long made him my best critic and the only person I can always show a first draft to. I am also grateful for his feminism, his support, and his wit, but more than anything I am grateful for our dear and enduring friendship, a friendship which began seventeen years ago and which still threads itself, like a pathway, into the future.

Preface: Criticism and History

According to bourgeois literature, the important events of history are the events of inner history. Suffering is portrayed as a personal struggle, experienced by the individual in isolation. Alienation becomes a heroic disease, for which there is no social remedy. Irony masks resignation to a situation one cannot alter or control. The human situation is seen as static, with certain external forms varying but the eternal anguish remaining. Every political system is perceived to set some small group into power, so that changing the identity of the group will not affect our "real" (that is, private) lives. If the work of literature does not make these notions sufficiently explicit, the critic helps to locate them in their context of "universals." Thus simply expressed, the elements of bourgeois ideology have a clear role in maintaining the status quo. Arising out of a system that functions through corporate competition for profits, the ideas of the bourgeoisie imply the ultimate powerlessness of the individual, the futility of public action, and the necessity of despair.

—Lillian Robinson,
Sex, Class, and Culture, 1978

This book came out of a course I taught at La Salle College in the spring of 1974. It was not a successful course. In fact, it was a course so charged with tensions and small animosities that I exhausted my store of therapies—small groups, conferences, and compromises—without ever really resolving any of them. As an indication of how this made me feel, I will tell you the line that I seized on (in another account of feminist teaching) and that played through my mind during the three and a half months of that long and intractable semester: it went "sometimes I felt like leaving town."

In many ways, of course, the class was soothingly—and

deliberately—traditional. It was only the second women's studies course to be proposed, as a "special topic," in the English Department of a Roman Catholic college which had become coed four years before, and as a means to getting the course taught I felt I bore the weight of making it sound "respectable." The title, "A Room of Their Own: Women Writers of Eighteenth, Nineteenth, and Twentieth-Century Britain," was at least overtly benign. Now, in fact, it suggests nothing so much as a genteel ghetto, three centuries of female authors scribbling away in back bedrooms or seldom-used parlors—who could object to a course on female writers so unobtrusive in their authorship as that? The writers, moreover, were all strategically "major," at least for women—at the time that I taught this class our course on Major Authors included only males—and each of the novels taught was about a young girl growing up, a conventional plot, familiar from novels about young men and promising the possibility of discreet comparisons and contrasts. Most of the works were also partially autobiographical, but this fact did not win any particular seal of approval, and I believe I made some point, in an early prospectus, about looking first at letters for one account of an author's life and then at fiction, presumably for a very different one—as if literature and life, though related, had been carefully put up in different jam jars. Finally, and privately, I had chosen novels written between 1778 and 1952 with the intention of examining the relation between literature and historical development, but this was not an objective to which I drew attention in my efforts to get the course taught.

I had not intended to look at power, especially covert power, in these novels, and that I ended up doing so appeared to me at the time to have come about by accident—that semester it seemed alternately a lucky break and a nasty collision. Both a preoccupation with power and subtle power strategies on the part of the authors simply presented themselves to me—like unlooked-for patterns in a carpet, the startling figure of a fist, say, raised at repeated intervals among the peonies. To a full three-quarters of my class, however, English majors who were not yet feminist, the figure would not appear, and when I persisted in tracing its outlines I appeared perverse and, even worse, I appeared "political." (This was before I learned to begin every course by talking about the politics of criticism.) *Evelina*, for example, struck three-quarters of the class as a "funny book," and when I suggested that Frances Burney both accepted and resented the conventions of the marriage market, that she invited us both to laugh at and to feel the insult of Evelina's various kidnappings, violations, and assaults, I seemed confusing, overly serious, and unreasonable. When I maintained that Burney not only took Evelina's violations seriously but that she endowed her heroine with subtle retaliatory powers, I made them angry. To more than half the class my deconstruction of the text seemed the *real* violation, and that the feminist quarter of the class went along with my assaults only proved, once and for all, that feminist politics operated as a kind of mind-altering drug.

It was a year before I worked on the material I had taught in that class, and then I wrote an essay, in six weeks, on covert power in *Evelina*.[1] I was exercising a form of self-therapy this time around, a quick show of tightrope walking to prove that I hadn't lost my balance. Not much later, of course, what appeared to have been individual if not eccentric footwork with these texts revealed itself to have been so many strides in a collective motion. For somewhere in the early seventies feminist scholars in several disciplines, and I among them, had shifted focus. We had relinquished "woman as victim" for "women as agents of change," and our previous examination of women's "debilitating limitations" had given way to an exploration of their "persisting power."[2] In 1974, for example, the year I happened upon covert power, anthropologists Michelle Zimbalist Rosaldo and Louise Lamphere—in the introduction to their anthology *Woman, Culture, and Society*—asserted that "women have had a good deal more power than conventional theorists have assumed,"[3] and in the fall of 1975 Barbara Bellow Watson published "On Power and the Literary Text," in which she suggested that "literature has more to say about power than might at first appear . . . literature teaches that power is relative and confused; that power is everywhere in a variety of forms and degrees; that all our formulations about power are too simple."[4]

In 1976 Berenice Carroll's *Liberating Women's History* included several essays in which feminist historians self-consciously reversed "the present emphasis upon the utter, total, and complete victimization of women in the past" and replaced it with an emphasis on women's power or agency: "The true history of women is the history of their ongoing functioning in that male-defined world, *on their own terms*."[5] Then, in the spring of 1977, in a review article on women's history, Carolyn Lougee wrote that "a theme emerging both in theoretical discussion and in empirical studies is the need to recognize within the context of seemingly debilitating limitations placed upon women in European societies the persisting power of women; the integrity of their choices; and their participation in the definition of roles, values, and behavior."[6]

At the same time, women's power became the official topic of scholarly feminist gatherings. In April 1976 the Pioneers for Century III Conference focused on women's power, and in November 1977 the Maryland Women's History Conference was called "Women and Power: Dimensions of Women's Historical Experience."[7] More subtly and more slowly, allusions to change and power appeared in the titles, and examinations of power in the content, of literary books: *The Female Imagination* (1972) and *Relative Creatures* (1974) were followed by *Literary Women* (1976), *A Lit-*

erature of Their Own (1977), *The Resisting Reader* (1977), and *Communities of Women* (1978).[8]

In the process of adjusting our sights from woman's oppression to women's agency, we began to conceive of power somewhat differently. Definitions were expanded, and power as control, a particularly masculine form of power, got less attention for a change than power as ability, a resource more available to women: "The definition of power as dominance covers one range of uses. The definition of power as ability, competence, and the closely related definition of power as energy, cover another, much wider and more interesting cluster of meanings."[9] Power, finally, was discovered where only oppression had stood before, in masked forms and unlooked-for places, in "women's experience of their separateness from men," in women's culture, and in women's sphere: ". . . not only the separate occupations, status, experiences, and rituals of women but also their separate consciousness, which internalizes patriarchal assumptions."[10] In fact, a recent review article on feminist scholarship suggested that "the earlier simplification of the 'bad old days' is in danger of being replaced by an equally distorted view of Victorian America as an era of female power and sisterly utopia."[11] By the spring of 1980 some feminist scholars appeared to have come full circle.

But, whether circular or not, why did this refocusing take place, and what, after all, does it matter? These are not questions I can definitively answer, but they are questions I think it important to ask—lest the collective strides of feminist scholars appear themselves to be a kind of privatized dance. Perhaps the shift from victim to agent, from oppression to power, is related to two seemingly opposite experiences on the part of many feminists, experiences which have their root in that larger women's movement to which feminist scholarship belongs. On the one hand, the shift might be attributed to the sense of gain and of increased power experienced by women in the early seventies. In the words of Judy

Stacey, "many of us began to take our lives, our work, ourselves more seriously and to expand our individual and collective ambitions and many of us for the first time. We made and were making basic changes in our lives and there was a headiness about it as well and an internalization of the process. We began to identify with other images of female potency historically, cross culturally." But, on the other hand, the early to mid seventies were also a time of loss, a time when we began to develop a renewed and more sophisticated sense of our own impotency. The movement as we knew it seemed to have peaked and was beginning to encounter the serious backlash it has provoked. We began to perceive the profundity of female opposition to feminism, and the divisions among women as well. "I think this made it less possible to see women simply as victims. Women were often actively defending their 'oppressed' conditions. It forced some of us to develop broader definitions of women's power and agency. It made us more aware of a dialectic of power that wasn't simply male/female, oppressor/victim."[12]

In the context of this growing backlash especially, the emphasis on women's oppression began to seem discouraging—not merely to our feminist students, who complained publicly that the focus on victimization was depressing, but also to ourselves, who privately agreed. The emphasis on universal and persisting limitation seemed to lead to the conclusion that, in the words of Sheila Johansson, "for one half of humanity, time has meant nothing more than survival, or a cowlike submission to inscrutable natural processes and outrageous social customs." If the history of women's lives was in fact the chronicle of a timeless and unchanging oppression, then we too were doomed. As individuals, as a movement, we needed a stronger heritage than that. Thus, half in strategy, we turned to the past, hoping to find "traditions of protest and resistance" beyond those left to us by the women's rights movement.[13] Hoping to find them, we were prompted to ask different questions, and by asking different questions we began to find what we had been hoping for.

But women's power, as Nina Auerbach has observed, is a power that must be "searched out and insisted upon," and such insistence, even in the privacy of one's scholarship, even in the seclusion of one's classroom, is a form of struggle. It is, in fact, a form of resistance to distorting ideologies—to those values, images, and ideas which insure either that dominant social relations "are seen by most members of society as 'natural' or not seen at all."[14] It was, in part, an ideology about women's power, about the unnaturalness of power as a subject and as an activity for genteel (and major) female writers, which made it difficult and painful for three-quarters of my women's studies class to see the figure in the carpet. And it was a sense that the natural design of things was being skewed which produced a ripple of tension among some of my colleagues when it was announced that I had received money from ACLS for studying women, power, and subversion. (In a very different vein, it was amusement at traditional order overturned which prompted my ex-husband to remark, with wry and self-reflecting humor, that this was "a funny book to dedicate to a man.")

But ideological barriers, unfortunately for our work, unfortunately for our lives, are not merely "out there"—where they are worrisome enough. They are within. The barriers were apparent in the year of silence that elapsed between the difficulties of my class and the determined wit of my article on *Evelina*, and they surfaced again a year later while I was finding subversive power in Jane Austen, thinking—more lightheartedly than my class three years before—"this can't be! I must be going mad!" And once again the private, the presumably peculiar, is part of a larger context and seen within that context assumes a wider meaning than before.

Writing in 1979, Barbara Haber pointed to an ideological

tension over women's power when she suggested that feminists on the left had abandoned a critique of modern family life and that they had done so in part out of "feminine guilt at putting ourselves first." Writing in 1975, Florence Howe maintained that "power has been anathema to the women's movement" as a whole: "The movement has not only attempted to be tactful; it has also tended to operate within the boundaries created by its own state of oppression. That oppression has taught women certain techniques for survival, among them the idea of cultivating their own garden, without infringing on male territory. To a significant extent, this has been the history of women through the past two centuries of struggle."[15]

What both suggest is that old ideologies persist and that it is necessary to encounter and explore their operation in our politics, in our private lives, and in our work. It is an ideological tension we still feel about power and power relations, for example, which helps explain our focus on the past—and which ties us to the very women whom we study. As Sarah Stage has observed, women's studies owes its impetus to the contemporary women's movement, but its greatest energies have been devoted not to illuminating the present or the immediate past but to examining issues of female sexuality and women's sphere in the nineteenth century.[16] And is only in part, I think, that we wish to uncover a heritage that has been lost, for to study power and powerlessness in nineteenth-century female life is also to employ a strategy. It is to explore power where we can do so in relative tranquillity; it is to examine power struggles where we can work without having to work through a bad case of nerves.

Still, to examine power in the past is also to clarify the present. It is to work out models with which to assess, and to change, our own condition. It is a political, if also a strategic, act. To "search out and insist upon" women's power in the past, moreover, with the intention of insisting on our own, is to do more than tilt with mere ideas. "The realm of the mind" is not "some abstract Agora where ideas duel gracefully among themselves all unconscious of whose interests they serve," though it has been convenient for the operation of our society for us to believe that this is so.[17] To insist upon women's power in the past, and in the present, is to challenge the most dominant and most entrenched of social relations, and the radical nature of this resistance may be measured by the massiveness of the forces which are gathered now against the women's movement. The anti-Equal Rights, antiabortion, antigay movements represent a highly coordinated, well-financed, and potentially massive attempt to destroy the gains made by the feminist movement. Behind this attempt lie the fear of women's power and women's independence and the determination to crush both. As in mid-nineteenth-century Britain, moreover, a conservative ideology about women is being reconsolidated not only as a means of keeping women in their place but as a means of mitigating and offsetting economic crisis. Indeed the effort to restore male control of women's bodies and of the family as a whole may be seen as part of a more general attempt by big business to dismantle the welfare state, to redirect funds for social needs into the private sector, and to reprivatize what had been made public through the struggles of women and of the working class.[18]

It is within contexts such as these that our acts of feminist scholarship take place—and it is finally within these contexts that we must assess our labors. Why write on strategies of power in writers of the past, and how is that to serve the better interest of the present? One answer, surely, is that studies of nineteenth-century women writers, by sorting out for us how women have experienced ideology in the past, may help us clarify our situation in the present, may help deliver us from ideological illusion. But such unravelings to be helpful must be complex. They must work through the tangled skeins of the historically specific, and they must see the individual always in the larger context, for it is this larger context which tells us what the private, the seemingly isolated, has really been.

Now this, it seems to me, is precisely the kind of work which feminist literary criticism is inclined to do. As I write, indeed, I am a conscious participant in a collective movement, a movement born itself by being aware. For our experience of the magnitude and the complexity of the forces against us in the present seems to be prompting still another alteration in our reading of the past: a renewed sense not only that it is women's power as well as their oppression which we must explore but that it is not "woman" we are exploring but women and that to see women we must see men, that to see gender we must also see heterosexism, race, and class, that to examine the force of ideologies we must examine the social relations which they insure, that "it is precisely the *interactions* between women's sphere(s) and the 'rest' of history that enable us to discover women's contributions to world history and the meaning of their subjection."[19]

As literary critics in America, however, we will find that this welding of text and context in itself requires a contest—with ideology and with the dominant relations which that ideology sustains:

> For the dominant ideology of Western countries is clearly that Anglo-American empirical realism for which all dialectical thinking represents a threat and whose mission is essentially to serve as a check on social consciousness. . . . The method of such thinking . . . consists in separating reality into air-tight compartments, carefully distinguishing the political from the economic, the legal from the political, the sociological from the historical [and the literary from everything but itself] so that the full implications of any problem can never come into view; and in limiting all statements to the discrete and the immediately verifiable, in order to rule out any spec-

> ulative and totalizing thought which might lead to a vision of social life as a whole.[20]

It is this ideology which Lillian Robinson has in mind when she writes that modernism, as the dominant form of literary criticism in America, "seeks to intensify isolation," that it "forces the work of art, the artist, the critic outside of history," that it thereby denies "the possibility of understanding ourselves as *agents* in the material world, for all has been removed to an abstract world of ideas, where interactions can be minimized or emptied of real meaning and real consequences."[21] It is this ideology which feminist literary criticism in particular, and ideological criticism as a whole, is suited to encounter and to overcome, and it is one project of this book to be part of that collective labor. Certainly the effort must be undertaken if we are to see the meaning of the individual life, the private difficulty, the isolated text, if we are to achieve a vision of social life as a whole, and if we are to make that vision serve not the interests of an exploitative, sexist, homophobic, and racist social order but the better interests—of struggle and of change.

J.L.N.

Introduction

Power and the Ideology of "Woman's Sphere"

. . . women, in their position in life, must be content to be inferior to men; but as their inferiority consists chiefly in their want of power, this deficiency is abundantly made up to them by their capability of exercising influence.

—Sarah Ellis, *The Daughters of England*, 1845

. . . as with work on the lower classes, slave populations, and peasants, work on relations between the sexes makes the location of power a trickier business than when one is looking at governments, parties, factions, and clientage systems. Power can lodge in dangerous nooks and crannies.

—Natalie Zemon Davis, "'Women's History' in Transition," 1976

The powers of the weak are, finally, more powerful than we think and can only be ignored by the powerful at their peril.

—Elizabeth Janeway, "On the Power of the Weak," 1975

In April of 1850, when Elizabeth Gaskell confessed to Tottie Fox that "the discovery of one's exact work in the world is the puzzle: . . . I am sometimes coward enough to wish we were back in the darkness where obedience was the only seen duty of women,"[1] she was finding words for a private and personally troubling experience of a more general ideological crisis, a crisis of confidence over the status, the proper work, and the power of middle-class women. This crisis of confidence, which emerged in the 1830s and 1840s in Great Britain, took the form of a prolonged debate over the "woman question," a debate so extensive that in 1869 Frances Power Cobbe was provoked to remark that "of all theories concerning women, none is more curious than the theory that it is needful to make a theory about them. . . . We are driven to conclude," she continues, that while men grow like trees "women run in moulds, like candles, and we can make them long-threes or short-sixes, whichever we please."[2]

The debate over the "woman question," in addition to its mass production of theories about women's "mission," "kingdom," or "sphere," gave an emphasis to the subject of women's power, and in particular to their influence, which was historically unprecedented. One has only to take manuals addressed to genteel women in the late eighteenth century and lay them alongside those written for middle-class women some sixty to seventy years later to see a deepening tension over women's power begin to manifest itself like footprints in a flower garden. In 1774, for example, in *A Father's Legacy to His Daughters*, John Gregory makes very few allusions to the power or influence of women. Although women are recognized as having been designed to "soften [the] hearts and polish [the] manners" of men, Gregory is less interested in the power women have to redeem men than charmed by the facility with which they please them. Woman's sphere, therefore, is not conceived of as the locus of a particular influence. Genteel women in Gregory's *Legacy* are "companions and equals" of men, rational beings, and their separate world is recommended not because it affords them power but because it lends them scope in which to be rationally human, in which to exercise "good sense and good taste."[3]

Twenty years later, however, James Fordyce makes many references to women's influence. One of his first *Sermons to Young Women* is "on the Importance of the Female Sex, especially the Younger Part," and in it he reassures women that a "principal source of your importance is the very great and extensive influence which you in general have with our sex." Genteel women have more extensive tasks in Fordyce than to polish manners and instill decency: they are to "promote general reformation" among men. And their separate sphere is important less as a realm in which they may demonstrate good taste than as a dominion in which they exercise a specific potency: "There is an influence, there is an empire which belongs to you . . . I mean that which has the heart as its object."[4]

By 1798 Thomas Gisborne, in *An Enquiry into the Duties of the Female Sex*, feels prompted to remind women not only that they have "influence" but that its effects are "various and momentous" and that this influence, like the power of men, extends to society as a whole. Thus, genteel women are urged to consider "the real and deeply interesting effects which the conduct of their sex will always have on the happiness of society." But the insistence upon women's influence reaches a culmination some thirty years later when Sarah Ellis begins *The Women of England* (1839) by declaring both that women's influence is social in nature and that it is in some ways more socially significant than the power of men: "You have deep responsibilities; you have urgent claims; a nation's moral worth is in your keeping."[5]

This same tension and counterinsistence in relation to women's power leave traces on periodical literature addressed to the "woman question." In 1810, for example, an author for the *Edinburgh Review* makes only one reference to women's influence, giving far more emphasis to the dignity, the delightfulness, and the ornamental quality of women's character and to the importance of their personal happiness. But by 1831, in literature of the same kind, power and influence are frequent subjects of concern, and references to both are accompanied by a sharpening distinction between what is appropriate to women and what to men. Most authors—and it is worth noting that much of this literature was written by men—reject the notion that women have power, but they acknowledge and give value to the fact that women possess "enormous," "immense," or "vast" "influence." This influence, of course, is always reassuringly unobtrusive, "secret," "unobserved," an "undercurrent below the surface."[6]

In 1833 a writer for *Fraser's Magazine*, who is actually defending the female character, is still obliged to doubt the existence of amazons, though he admits that there are many instances of "females acting in a body in defence of their homes." In 1841 an author for the *Edinburgh Review* dismisses the proposition that men and women will ever be equal "in power and influence upon the affairs of the world" and warns, rather ill-naturedly, that if women "be made ostensibly powerful . . . the spirit of chivalry . . . will speedily cease." But women do have "immense influence," he concedes, and that influence must "be allowed to flow in its natural channels, namely domestic ones." In the same year a writer for the *Westminster Review* admits that "power" as encoded in laws seems "permanent and transmittable in nature, while influence dies with the possessor," but women, he concludes hopefully, do not *want* power in the first place: ". . . the peculiar duties of women are guarded by instincts and feelings more powerful than the desire for political power."[7]

This valorization of women's influence, it should be clear, was aimed at devaluing actions and capacities which we can only call other forms of power, and, in this way, the peddling of women's influence, in a sort of ideological marketplace, functioned to sustain unequal power relations between middle-class women and middle-class men. Having influence, in fact, having the ability to persuade others to do or to be something that was in *their* own interest, was made contingent upon the renunciation of such self-advancing forms of power as control or self-definition. To have influence, for example, the middle-class woman was urged to relinquish self-definition; she was urged to become identified by her services to others, in particular to men:

> . . . men in general are more apt than women, to act and think as if they were created to exist of, and by, themselves; and this self-sustained existence a wife can only share, in proportion as she is identified in every thing with her husband.
>
> It is necessary for her to lay aside all her natural caprice, her love of self-indulgence, her vanity, her indolence—in short, her very *self*—and assuming a new nature, which [is] to spend her mental and moral capabilities in devising means for promoting the happiness of others, while her own derives a remote and secondary existence from theirs.[8]

Having influence also required women to lay aside any desire for the power to achieve, especially outside the domestic sphere, for "it is from an ambitious desire to extend the limits of this sphere, that many have brought trouble upon themselves." And even within the home, achievement must be circumscribed. The possession of talent is "the possession of a dangerous heritage—a jewel which cannot with propriety be worn." Most centrally, of course, the power of control must be renounced, and Sarah Ellis apologizes for suggesting that women "preside" even in the home, being "aware that the word *preside*, used as it is here, may produce a startling effect upon the ear of man." To have influence, in effect, meant doing without self-definition, achievement, and control, meant relinquishing power for effacement of the self in love and sacrifice: "All that has been expected to be enjoyed from the indulgence of selfishness, must then of necessity be left out of our calculations, with all that ministers to the pride of superiority, all that gratifies the love of power, all that converts the woman into the heroine."[9]

The preoccupation with women's power that leaves its mark on nineteenth-century manuals and on other literature addressed to the "woman question" reappears like a bold thread in the texture of the works in this study. But it is significant that the heroines of these works, Evelina, Elizabeth Bennet, Lucy Snowe, and Maggie Tulliver, are generally endowed not with power as influence but with power as ability and that Burney, Austen, Brontë, and Eliot give evidence of that "love of power . . . that converts the woman into the heroine." Indeed, it is one of the characteristic strategies of these authors to subvert masculine control and male domination in their novels by quietly giving emphasis to female capability, as if the pattern in the background of an embroidered piece had been subtly worked into relief.

One form of ability, for example, is autonomy, the power of being one's own person, and being one's own person is multiply and often subtly defined. It may mean having one's private opinions—Evelina's letters are full of unflattering observations about men—or it may take the shape of self-defending actions—Evelina refuses a dance partner against the rules; Elizabeth deftly rejects Darcy's proposal. Women are also made powerful in these novels by being endowed with the capacity to achieve, to perform tasks, to act not merely on other individuals but on situations, and although the scope of achievement is more limited in female characters than in male—Madame Beck makes a success of a school for girls but not of being an industrial capitalist—the emphasis given to achievement as power is used in *Villette,* as in other works, to balance or even to outweigh the power of male characters and so to alter what we *feel* in the course of reading the novel about the traditional divisions of power between women and men. Some women writing fiction, it appears, having found it unthinkable, unrealistic, or unhealthy to give their female characters such traditionally masculine power as the power of control, managed to make women *seem* powerful, nevertheless, by giving emphasis and value to power as capacity.

In choosing to focus on female ability, of course, these writers themselves exercised a form of agency, of resistance to dominant values. In their foregrounding of female ability and in their subversive undercutting of male control, they illustrate what Elizabeth Janeway has maintained: even "a withdrawal of attention . . . a concentration on other areas" are "ways in which the weak exercise their power."[10] The ability of female characters and the power strategies of their creators, however, are difficult at first to see, and part of the difficulty at least lies in our own cultural limitations. Our very definitions of power—like our conceptions of "history" or of "art"—have been deformed by traditions which have systematically excluded women. In all fields of women's studies, therefore, our shift in focus from the limitations of women's situation to the reality of their persisting power has raised questions about what power really is. It has committed us both to broadened definitions of power and to a certain openness, to an acknowledgment of the idea that female power "can lodge in dangerous nooks and crannies."[11]

Berenice Carroll, for example, has reminded us that the definition of power primarily as "control, dominance, and influence" is of recent origin and that the primary meaning of power as late as 1933 was "ability, energy, and strength." Power, according to Carroll, has been defined not just as control but also as "ability," as the capacity to assert "one's will over one's body, one's own organs and functions and over the physical environment—a power which is seen as inherently satisfying and not merely as an instrument to other ends, as neither requiring nor leading to the power to command obedience in other persons."[12] Power as ability, that is, has been defined both as achievement and competence and, by implication, as a form of self-definition or self-rule. It is this power of ability or capability that seams together the fiction I am going to explore.

Of course, power in women's fiction may also be difficult to see because power is a subject and a capacity which make women writers ill at ease, and uneasiness breeds disguise or, at the least, obliqueness. In the eighteenth and nineteenth centuries, in particular, the act of writing in itself appeared to lend women a self-assertiveness which seemed out of keeping with properly feminine aspirations. Elaine Showalter suggests that the ambivalence which many women writers felt toward the self-revelation and assertion necessary to writing fiction prompted a whole spectrum of defensive strategies which ranged from the use of male pseudonyms to the punishment of aspiring heroines to the author's insistence in private life on the conventionality of her own womanhood. More recently, Sandra Gilbert and Susan Gubar have isolated a pervasive "anxiety of authorship—a radical fear that she cannot create, that because she can never become a 'precursor' the act of writing will isolate or destroy her" as a crucial mark of women's literary subculture in the nineteenth century.[13] To write at all and then to write of power, perhaps to perform some transforming action in one's fiction upon traditional power divisions, was surely to multiply defensive strategies, and in *Evelina, Pride and Prejudice, Villette,* and *The Mill on the Floss* the ability of female characters and the power strategies of their creators are systematically disguised, offset, or explained into moonshine. Evelina's satirical strictures, for example, are excused by her innocence and by her ignorance of city ways, and Elizabeth Bennet's refreshing self-direction is qualified by her defensive ironies. She may speak her mind to Darcy, may finally change him, and the reader is allowed to enjoy her daring, but at the same time we are continually reminded that Elizabeth is wrong about Wickham and wrong about Darcy and that she is controlled by her desire to please both.

Although each of these novels, moreover, is the story of a quest, the story of entry into the world, of education, and of growth, including growth in power, the heroine's power is sometimes renounced and often diminished at the end of the novel, so that it seems that the work has had nothing to do with power at all.[14] For no matter how much force the heroine is granted at the beginning of her story, ideology, as it governed life and as it governed literary form, required that she should marry, and marriage meant relinquishment of power as surely as it meant the purchase of wedding clothes. Thus, Evelina gives up satire in the third volume of the novel in order to weep, faint, and otherwise prepare herself for the princely Orville, and Elizabeth Bennet, though her own woman to the end, still dwindles by degrees into the moral balance required in Darcy's wife. Even in *Villette* and *The Mill on the Floss*, where marriage plots are more totally resisted, resistance appears ultimately to exhaust authorial resources. The quest of Lucy Snowe ends abruptly with the death of Lucy's fiancé, and in *The Mill on the Floss* the unwed heroine drowns at the end of the novel.

As they wrote about quest and entry into the world these authors, it should be clear, felt the pressure of ideologies which required circumscription of power as rigorously as they required marriage (and more loss of power) as a "happy" ending. These are not difficulties with which male writers have had to wrestle, and it is the experience of these pressures, which are at once acceded to and rebelled against, that gives rise to the peculiar dominance in these novels of tension, disguise, and ultimately disjunctions of form. In any work, of course, it is not only what a text does say but what it does not say that reveals its relation to dominant images, ideas, and values. It is in the "significant *silences* of a text, in its gaps and absences, that the presence of ideology can be most positively felt."[15] But in these novels in particular, the very covertness of power, the nature and degree of its disguise, the very omission of overt reference are of the greatest interest, for subversion, indirection, and disguise are natural tactics of the resisting weak, are social strategies for managing the most intense and the most compelling rebellions.

In these specific novels, finally, the tensions created by each author's struggle with conventions—by her insistence on dealing with female power in the first place, her subversion of traditional power relations, her substitution of ability for influence, and her refusal, for the most part, totally to relinquish the heroine's ability at the end of the story—were surely intensified by the fact that each novel had an unusually direct origin in the author's own experience. Each writer, in fact, appears to be working through some painful personal encounter with culturally imposed patterns of male power and female powerlessness. In Burney this is specifically the shock of being reduced to merchandise in the marriage market. In Austen it is more generally the experience of being without money, without carriages, without options, the enduring experience of suffering restrictions upon her autonomy, and in Brontë and Eliot it is the external and internal limitations imposed on their passionate and half-guilty desire to achieve.

Taken together, then, these novels may be said to register a developing tension over women's power, a tension which appears to have been central to that general crisis of consciousness over the role and status of middle-class women which surfaced in the 1830s and 1840s. What is more significant, however, is that in their subversion of traditional power relations and ultimately in their substitution of female ability for feminine influence these novels delineate a line of covert, ambivalent, but finally radical resistance to the ideology of their day. Taken together, they seem to articulate what Raymond Williams has called an emergent "structure of feeling," a development of consciousness which is as yet embryonic, which is tied to dominant ideology, but which is nevertheless alternative or oppositional to dominant values, suggesting that the alternative to "received and produced fixed forms" is "not silence: not the absence, the unconscious, which bourgeois culture has mythicized. It is a kind of feeling and thinking which is indeed social and material, but each in an embryonic phase before it can become fully articulate and defined exchange."[16]

The line of resistance, moreover, grows bolder as the ideology of women's influence takes hold. Between Burney's *Evelina* in 1778 and Eliot's *The Mill on the Floss* in 1860, conceptions of male power in these novels are expanded so that women's power and the unequal power divisions between women and men become increasingly a matter of overt concern. Men's power in Burney almost always takes the form of force or control in social situations—of assault in ballrooms or ravishment in carriages. Power is the ability to impose one's self on another or to defend one's self from imposition. But in Eliot men's power is the ability not only to dominate others but to define the self and to achieve: ". . . you are a man, Tom, and have power, and can do something in the world."[17] That men have more power than women, therefore, is made more significant in *The Mill on the Floss* than in *Evelina*.

Between Burney and Eliot, too, unequal divisions of power are increasingly perceived or conceived of in these novels as imposed by the community rather than as natural or given. The community as a force, therefore, becomes more and more dominant—although its force may be mystified, as in *Villette*—and that development is accompanied by a growing tendency to portray community values as ideology and as ideology unwittingly internalized by the heroine. At the same time, however, the strategy of giving power to the heroine, the power of ability rather than of influence or control, becomes more and more pronounced and is expressed in the increasing emphasis given to quest—the development of the heroine and especially of her desire for power—at the expense of love. In Burney, for example, an incipient quest plot is simply abandoned to the love plot in the third volume, while in Austen love and quest are forced into an uneasy balance.

Taken together, then, these novels suggest more ways in which women's writing may be both the locus of compensating fantasies and the site of protest, actions expressive of the authors' power, and in this respect the following study develops a line of reading which feminist critics have begun to explore. Patricia Spacks, for example, has written of one woman artist that "her own power was the power to imagine what she wished of others . . . to recreate her experience in a way that made it tolerable." Ellen Moers has written of the gothic and of factory novels as the locus of middle-class women's displaced protest of their lot. Elaine Showalter has suggested several ways in which a subculture of female writers was informed by covert ways of dramatizing the inner life, by fantasies of "money, mobility, and power." Nina Auerbach has explored fictional communities of women as the continuing source of female strength. And most recently Sandra Gilbert and Susan Gubar have posited a whole tradition among female writers of creating "submerged meanings, meanings hidden within or behind the more accessible, 'public' content of their works," so that the works "are in some sense palimpsestic, works whose surface designs conceal or obscure deeper, less accessible (and less socially acceptable) levels of meaning." Each of these critics works helpfully and fertilely within the assumption that "art enables men and women both to order, interpret, mythologize or dispose of their own experience."[18]

But most studies of subversive strategies in women's fiction have tended to focus on the presence of unchanging or transhistorical patterns or have tended to isolate the text not just from developing material conditions but from shifting ideologies as well, and this tendency to universalize has led many of us to claim, rather too easily, that art is a transforming action upon history without our having to say in fact what that history has been. Susan Gubar and Sandra Gilbert, for example, while recognizing the reality of "male-dominated society" and of women's attempts to redefine their society along with their art, have focused their study on women's struggle against "patriarchal literary authority" and patriarchal images and conventions. Nina Auerbach, too, although she makes some striking connections between text and historical context, does not give emphasis to the changing ideological and material situations in which the evolution of literary myth takes place. My own work differs in that it attempts to trace the shifting historical situation in which literary redefinitions and evolutions unfolded.

Elaine Showalter, of course, does explore female literary traditions in the context of the "still-evolving relationships between women writers and their society," but where she has given us an overview of a female literary tradition my own aim has been to lay out paradigms of reading in which the complexities and ambiguities of the relation between novel and cultural context are central.[19] Indeed, it is one project of this study to suggest how works of women's fiction might be read in several contexts—in relation to the changing material conditions of women's lives, to the ideological representations and distortions of those conditions, to an author's particular biographical experience of these, and to the ideological content and shaping force of such conventions in women's fiction as the quest and the marriage plot. Following Terry Eagleton (more or less), I have assumed that a work of fiction presents itself to us less as "historical than as a sportive flight from history, a reversal and a resistance of history."[20] Although I make note of the way in which a text might be said to "evoke" historical situations,[21] I have dwelt on the way it relates itself to ideological perceptions or distortions of those situations. I have dwelt, that is, on the way a work of fiction relates itself to ideas, images, and values which insure that the situation in which one class has power over another and in which men have power over women is seen as natural or not seen at all. Specifically, I have asked how these works both support and resist ideologies which have tied middle-class women to the relative powerlessness of their lot and which have prevented them from having a true knowledge of their situation, but I have also tried to consider how ideologies governing middle-class women intersect with and are interdependent upon more general ideologies which sustain and legitimate the power of the male bourgeoisie in relation to society as a whole.

My aim, in this, has been first to read the text more fully, for to locate threads of rebellion in a text without articulating rather specifically what is being rebelled against is to see only part of the pattern in the text itself, and it is not fully to see the transforming significance—and the limitations—of the subversive themes, metaphors, or strategies which, with painstaking labor, have been discovered. To see a text in isolation from its historical conditions is not fully enough to answer the question "So what?"—a question which Lillian Robinson has posed as the hardest we can ask ourselves as critics. A second aim has been to understand the present by coming to better terms with our collective past. Implicit in my focus, for example, are the assumption that ideology has been central to women's oppression and the assumption that literature gives us a peculiarly revealing access to the way in which ideology has been experienced. Studying the relation of literature and ideology allows us to explore one area of what has been called "the emotional texture of life for individuals in the past . . ." "the existential consequences of occupying a particular social location . . ." "the structure of choices" which the situation of women afforded them.[22] In examining both the text's subversion of ideology and its adherence to it, moreover, we may come to some understanding of the degree to which female writers may have acted as agents or as arbiters of change, for works of fiction practice upon their readers, skew the angle of vision from which readers experience their relation to the real, the degree of confidence which they feel in traditional social relations. Most important, finally, it is in exploring the ways in which women have experienced ideology in the past that we may come to understand the outlines of its hold upon us in the present and so move closer to our own delivery from illusion.[23]

But to explore the relation of a text to ideology is to do more than examine its relation to ideas, for "it is not the consciousness of [men and women] that determines their being, but on the contrary, their social being that determines their consciousness."[24] To understand the significance of a text's relation to ideology one must also examine the material conditions, the real relations, the contradictions out of which that ideology emerged. Between 1774 and 1845, for example, the particular historical conditions which gave rise to the ideology of woman's sphere are partially and unreflectingly evoked by manuals addressed to genteel women. Between 1774 and 1845, that is, these manuals are informed by the presence of an interesting conjunction. Mounting references to women's influence are accompanied by more and more frequent allusions to a general discontent among genteel women with the limitations of their role and status and by a deepening consciousness of the fact that men of the middle orders are enjoying economic and social mobility. In 1774 Dr. Gregory betrays little consciousness of any troubling insignificance in women's domestic lot. If the handiwork of upper-middle-class women is of no more than "trifling" value, if its significance lies for the most part in its enabling them "to fill up, in a tolerably agreeable way, some of the many solitary hours you must necessarily pass at home," that is a fact which is to be taken for granted. By 1794, however, James Fordyce is far more conscious than Dr. Gregory of married and single women of the middle and upper middle classes who are feeling insignificant or discontent with their sphere. Fordyce, in fact, is apparently surrounded by women with complaints. He hears young women exclaiming that, "though God has given you capacities of intellectual improvement, men have denied you the opportunities of it," and the complaint is "a very common one, and very popular with your sex." Four years later Gisborne begins his *Enquiry* by admitting that the "sphere of domestic life . . . admits far less diversity of action, and consequently of temptation, than is found in the widely differing professions and employments" of men, and he suggests that genteel young women in general complain that "the sphere in which women are destined to move, is so humble and so limited, as neither to require nor reward assiduity." By 1839 dissatisfaction with their lot appears so endemic to ordinary women of the middle class, not just to "masculine" grumblers, that

Ellis is moved to begin her manual on a note of sweeping disapproval: ". . . the women of England are . . . less usefull, and less happy than they were." Domestic usefulness particularly is in decline, and the author complains that it is difficult even to praise such "quiet and unobtrusive virtues" as remain "without exciting a desire to forsake the homely household duties of the family circle to practise such as are more conspicuous, and consequently more productive of an immediate harvest of applause."[25]

Significantly, the growing fear—or the increasing evidence—that middle-class women were discontent with the limitations of their sphere is accompanied in these manuals by a deepening awareness of the fact that middle-class men were making money and enjoying a social significance which they had not enjoyed before. In both Fordyce and Gisborne this emphasis on the discontent of women is accompanied by mounting references to the social significance of money among the middle classes, money earned, of course, by males. And in Ellis women's purported discontent with their lack of status is very frequently juxtaposed with a world in which money is everything, in which men are entirely devoted to efforts and calculations relating to their "pecuniary success."

What this unreflecting conjunction of references to female power, female discontent, and economic contradiction evokes is the causal relation between the "woman question" and what came to be perceived at least about the economic value of middle-class women between 1778 and 1860, a period which spans industrial takeoff and the establishment of bourgeois-class society—for the development of industrial capitalism did change the economic situation of middle-class women relative to that of middle-class men. Eric Hobsbawm, for example, notes that the "crucial achievement" of the industrial and French revolutions was that

> they opened careers to talent [the talent of middle-class men], or at any rate to energy, shrewdness, hard work, and greed.

> Not all careers, and not to the top rungs of the ladder, except perhaps in the USA. And yet, how extraordinary were the opportunities, how remote from the nineteenth century the static hierarchical ideal of the past! . . . in 1750 the son of a book binder would, in all probability, have stuck to his father's trade. Now he no longer had to. Four roads to the stars opened before him: business, education (which in turn led to the three goals of government, service, politics, and the free professions), the arts, and war.[26]

By the midnineteenth century the development of industrial capitalism had not led middle-class women along the same four roads. Indeed, although the absence of statistical data makes it difficult to compare women in preindustrial Britain with women of this later time, it has been argued that "industrialization far from emancipating women led to a contraction of some of their traditional functions in the economy—to a degree from which they have yet fully to recover." The nineteenth-century labor force, according to Eric Richards, was increasingly male-dominated, and "apart from domestic service, textiles, stitching, and washing there was little else open to women of any class in England before the final decades of the century."[27] The number of women employed in middle-class occupations, moreover, was even lower, for the trend toward employing women even in such spheres as shops, civil service, and business, all of which were open to men, did not begin until after 1870.[28]

At the same time, the recognized economic status of dependent married middle-class women also suffered a decline relative to the rising economic status of middle-class men, and the causes generally forwarded for what may be seen at least as a *shift in perception* are that, with the development of industrialization, home production of many household products declined; that household industries in which women and children worked alongside husbands and fathers also dwindled;[29] and that, as men's work separated further from the home, new definitions and perceptions of work were further developed, definitions and perceptions which made married women's work in the home less *visible* as work than it had been before.[30]

Literature on the "woman question," for example, makes frequent allusions to a decline in women's domestic labor and economic status, and, without claiming that this literature actually describes the middle-class woman's experience day to day, it is still possible to trace an indication of how women's domestic work was seen.[31] Thus in 1810 an article in the *Edinburgh Review* observes that "the time of women is considered worth nothing at all," and in 1841 the *Westminster Review* remarks that an "attendant effect of luxury and civilization is to procure leisure for the housekeeper as well as every body else. The greater perfection and division of labor procures for us all the necessaries and comforts of life almost ready made."[32] What some literature on the "woman question" also suggests is that this ostensible decline in women's economic activity and the recognized value of their work was linked with a decline in their status as well. In 1869, after remarking that "men have taken away from women the employments which formerly were appropriated to them," such as spinning, sewing, and domestic labors, one author goes on tó observe that

> when these and such like avocations were available to women of every rank, they were not only provided with subsistence, but they held that definite place in society and filled those recognized duties which placed them on a footing of substantial dignity, and forbade the raising of any question whether capacities were equal with those of men or not. Not intentionally, but actually, by the progress of science and forms of social existence that position has been taken from women.[33]

Unpaid domestic work lost visibility, then, at a time when it was not yet possible for middle-class women to enter the labor market in any equitable way, and the low status of women's work in the labor market must have enforced the low status of women's work in the home—and vice versa. At the same time, the rising economic and social power of middle-class men gave increasing value to work that was to be done by males, work that was at once public, divorced from the home, and salaried. All this was bound to have an effect on women's status as it also had on their sense of power,[34] and it is largely these economic and social contradictions which gave rise to an ideological crisis in which questions about women's status, power, and influence were central. Indeed, the establishment by the midnineteenth century of an ideological emphasis on women's influence was largely an attempt to resolve this economic contradiction and to maintain the subordination of middle-class women to middle-class men, an attempt to keep the lid on middle-class women by assuring them that they *did* have work, power, and status after all.

The ideology of woman's sphere, however, was also established at a time when industrial capitalism was beset both by economic crisis and by working-class unrest. The progress of industrial capitalism, according to Eric Hobsbawm, was far from smooth, and by the 1830s and 1840s it "produced major problems of growth not to mention revolutionary unrest unparalleled in any other period of recent British history." Working-class consciousness, in fact, came into existence between 1815 and 1848, more especially around 1830, shortly before the new ideology of woman's sphere emerged. As in America, the ideology of woman's sphere in Britain may be said to have "enlisted women in their domestic roles to absorb, palliate, and even to redeem the strain of social and economic transformation."[35] Women, in their isolation from competitive economic practices, were to act as the conscience of bourgeois society and through their influence over men mitigate the harshness of an industrial capitalist world. Woman's sphere, therefore, was defined as the "intellectual education of childhood, the moral guidance of youth, the spiritual influence over the home and society,

[and] the softening of relations between class and class which bind those together by deeds of love whom the material interests keep apart."[36] In reality, of course, "the canon of domesticity did not directly challenge the modern organization of work and pursuit of wealth. Rather, it accommodated and promised to temper them."[37] The ideology of woman's sphere, that is, served the interests of industrial capitalism by insuring the continuing domination of middle-class women by middle-class men and, through its mitigation of the harshness of economic transition, by insuring the continuing domination of male bourgeoisie in relation to working-class men and women as a whole.

The development of industrial capitalism, then, between *Evelina* and *The Mill on the Floss* empowered middle-class men, economically and socially, while it was *felt* at least to have disempowered middle-class women, and the development of this economic contradiction, of the ideological crisis which it provoked, and the attempts at ideological resolution which accompanied both inform and shape the women's fiction I am going to explore. Indeed, in these novels an emergent and rebellious structure of feeling about inequities of power between women and men is accompanied by a more and more overt evocation—and resentment—of economic inequities as well. Power divisions, for example, are linked with increasing explicitness to differences in economic function. Thus in *Evelina* Burney scorns money consciousness by projecting it onto the vulgar lower classes, but in *Pride and Prejudice* Austen draws attention to a relation between money and power before silently subverting it. In *Villette* access to work that pays is persistently felt to be the most fundamental source of power, although Brontë may be said to present the connection without making it fully articulate, and in *The Mill on the Floss* Eliot analytically evokes what Burney, Austen, and Brontë have either unreflectingly grasped or only partially presented. In *The Mill on the Floss* the division between men's and women's recognized economic functions is the major determinant of their power. And much of the first half of the novel is devoted to analyzing how that relation determines the lives of Tom and Maggie Tulliver.

Protest against power inequities between women and men, moreover, as expressed in the increasing emphasis given to quest and in the ever more determined resistance to conventional marriage plots, is brought into conjunction with buried protest first against class division and ultimately against capitalist development itself. Indeed the relation of each work to an ideology about women also locates it in relation to general ideologies about class division and ultimately about industrial capitalist relations. Burney, for example, endorses the class power of landed men in order to sustain a courtly ideology about genteel women, while Austen's endorsement of Elizabeth's independence is of a piece with her endorsement of economic individualism in middle-class men. Brontë's bitter resentment of the inequities of money between middle-class women and middle-class men leads to mystified protest on behalf of all those who are "creatures of shadow" rather than "creatures of sunshine," and Eliot's analysis of male and female socialization sees industrial capitalist development as dangerous, if not to the working class, at least to middle-class women.

What might appear at first to be relatively simple resistance to the ideology of woman's sphere therefore takes on, in this larger context, a wider significance; resistance to an ideology governing middle-class women intersects with resistance to ideologies sustaining capitalist relations as a whole, and it is this intersection which helps explain the radical content and finally the radical curtailment of rebellious strategies for women in these novels—an argument if there ever was one for looking at gender in relation to class. For protest of women's powerlessness is disconcerting enough. When it leads—intuitively and half consciously—to resentment of the economic inequities between women and men and to distaste for capitalist ethics and capitalist economic relations as a whole, rebellion becomes far more frightening and much more difficult to sustain, a fact which has its effect on the shape of these novels. What might be seen, that is, as a growth of consciousness that is potentially revolutionary—an emergent feeling on the part of the authors that power divisions are imposed rather than natural and a mounting resistance to those divisions in their fiction—does not in fact find satisfactory expression in their art. In these novels growing resistance produces growing tension, and the tension becomes particularly acute as, historically, the ideology of women's influence and ideologies sustaining industrial capitalism are established. The heroine's, and the author's, rebellion is not abandoned, but it is directed into fantasies of power which are increasingly apparent as fantasies and increasingly difficult to sustain. In Brontë and in Eliot, indeed, the authors themselves seem patently disbelieving.

The thrust of this tension, however, is not toward resignation so much as toward further covertness and further disguise, and this indicates at once the force with which ideology inhibits and the persistence with which women rebelled. Their rebelliousness, moreover, is more than a brand of false consciousness, for if on the one hand subversive writing defuses the desire for power by satisfying the longing for it, on the other subversive writing is itself an action upon one's readers and one's world. It is not only socialist novels which can destroy "conventional illusions" about human relations. Any novel may do so when it "shakes the optimism of the bourgeois world, when it casts doubt on the eternal nature of existing society, even if the author does not propose answers, even though [she] might not openly take sides."[38] To write subversively is more than a means of exercising influence. It is a form of struggle—and a form of power.

1. *Evelina*

To read this history of a young lady's entrance into the world is to read a chronicle of assault: for having made her debut in "public company," amid a round of London's most "fashionable Spring Diversions," Burney's genteel young heroine finds that she can go but few places indeed without being forced, intruded upon, seized, kidnapped, or in some other way violated by a male.[1] At her first assembly she is provoked by the "negligent impertinence" of a fop, at her second "tormented . . . to death" by a baronet.[2] A trip to the opera marks her first kidnapping, an evening at the play a public attack. At the Pantheon a lord affronts her by staring; at Vauxhall "gentlemen" "rudely" seize upon and pursue her; and at Marylebone, when she loses her party and her way, she finds that her distress "only furnished a pretence for impertinent witticisms" on the part of "bold and unfeeling" males (181, 218). Burney's *Evelina*, in fact, presents us with a world dominated by the imposition of men upon women, a world in which male control takes the form of assault, and a world in which male assault is the most central expression of power.

That the author of *Evelina*, herself a young woman of good family, should give this emphasis to male control, that she should portray male control as violation, and that she should virtually equate a young lady's entry into the world with her subjection to abuse expresses something pointed about the situation of genteel unmarried women in 1778. It evokes the fact that the status of young middle-class women was in doubt; it suggests that men felt a special authority to impose their will upon them; and it implies that respectable unmarried women were essentially powerless to avoid if not to resist this imposition. *Evelina,* in fact, evokes Burney's own experience of this general historical situation, for in 1775, only one year before she wrote the major part of her novel, Fanny Burney suffered what might be termed a species of male assault upon her status and autonomy.

Burney was then twenty-three, self-educated, evidently destined for marriage, interested in love but harboring some distaste for the awkward rituals of courtship, and liable to feel, with a distinct sense of her own autonomy, that "upon the whole, the most dignified thing for an exalted female must be to die an old maid." She enjoyed, too, unusual freedom in disposing of her own time, "following my own vagaries which my papa never controls," and she had besides a sense of personal status and value. She served as amanuensis to the great Dr. Burney, and she was engaged in writing long and witty journal letters to an admiring Mr. Crisp: "Send me a minute Journal of every thing, and never mind their being trifles—trifles well-dressed, are excellent food, and your cookery is (with me) of established reputation."[3]

The Burney family, moreover, though it had humble connections, was at least uneasily genteel. If Dr. Burney was a mere music teacher, he was also a respected scholar with an Oxford degree, and though his family remained to some extent "such sort of people," he himself entered easily into the great world.[4] His was not a family either to worry about finance for, though money for dowries was not to be had, there were funds to send one of Fanny's brothers to Cambridge and two of her sisters to France, and Burney's diary is free of those allusions to economy which so dominate the letters of Jane Austen. It came, then, as a shock that, at twenty-three, Fanny should be pressured to place herself upon the market, should be urged to consider marrying a man she hardly knew and did not care for—and this chiefly for his money.

It was in May of 1775, shortly before her twenty-fourth birthday, that Fanny received a declaration of sorts from a Mr. Barlow, an unremarkable young man whom she had met at tea four days before and whom—it is hardly surprising—she was eager to refuse: "I am too spoilt," she wrote, "by such men as my father and Mr. Crisp to content myself with a character merely inoffensive. I should expire of fatigue with him."[5] But Dr. Burney had several daughters without dowries, and Fanny, to her dismay, was urged by her sister, her grandmother, her maiden aunts, and her dear friend Daddy Crisp to consider the economics of her situation—Mr. Barlow too appeared provokingly "sanguine" at first about her acceptance. Mr. Crisp, for example, after recommending what he had heard of Mr. Barlow's disposition, went on to "the grand object of enquiry," Mr. Barlow's fortune:

> Is he of any profession, or only of an independent fortune? is either, or both, sufficient to promise . . . a comfortable [income]? You may live to the age of your grandmother, and not meet with so valuable an offer. . . . Look round you, Fan; look at your aunts; *Fanny Burney* won't always be what she is now! Mrs. Hamilton once had an offer of £3,000-a-year, or near it; a parcel of young giggling girls laugh'd her out of it. The man, forsooth, was not quite smart enough, though otherwise estimable. Oh, Fan, this is not a marrying age, without a handsome Fortune! . . . Suppose you lose your father,—take in all chances. Consider the situation of an unprotected, unprovided woman![6]

The letter was well intended, but that Daddy Crisp, a model of gentility and a sort of father-monitor as well, should ask her to consider a man she did not know and could not love, and all for the sake of an establishment, obviously pained Fanny and took her by surprise: "[Mr. Crisp] has written me such a letter! God knows how I shall answer it! Every body is against me but my beloved father." And then, perhaps a week later, Dr. Burney joined the cause, spoke to her "in favour of Mr. Barlow," and urged her not to be "peremptory" in her answer. The effect was devastating: Fanny felt assailed yet powerless to resist:

> I was terrified to death. I felt the utter impossibility of resisting not merely my father's *persuasion*, but even his advice. . . . I wept like an infant, when alone; ate nothing; seemed as if already married and passed the whole day in more misery than, merely on my own account, I ever did in my life, except [when a child] upon the loss of my own beloved mother, and ever revered and most dear grandmother![7]

The extent of her suffering, however, moved Dr. Burney to relent, and that very evening Fanny went to bed "light, happy, and thankful, as if escaped from destruction." On May 16 she wrote Daddy Crisp, asking forgiveness but maintaining that she was unable to act "from *worldly motives*," declaring herself "QUITE FIXED," and explaining that she had "long accustomed [herself] to the idea of being an old maid"; and so, for the most part, the affair of Mr. Barlow was ended.[8] But it could not have ended, one assumes, without leaving its trace, without putting Fanny in some doubt about the inviolability of her status and freedom. *Evelina*, which was written largely in the following year, gives all evidence of being a mode of coming to terms with this experience, the experience of being placed upon the market, the experience of being regarded with sanguinity by an unremarkable young man, the experience of being made to lose status and power—the experience, in short, of undergoing a species of assault.

What, in a general sense, lay behind this incursion upon Burney's status and autonomy was to a large degree the declining economic stature of genteel young women in the eighteenth century, for women of all stations had lost and were continuing to lose their previously recognized economic value. The working of household plots, the home production of household articles, the participation in family industry were all in decline, and the economic drift was to make women, especially women of the middle orders, more dependent economically upon men and men less recognizably dependent upon the domestic work of women. This decline in recognized economic value enforced women's traditionally subordinate position in relation to men, a phenomenon that did not go unnoticed by the age. Defoe, for one, understood that women's lower status went hand in hand with their loss of economic function, and he suggests that men took advantage of the situation: "They will not make them useful that they may not value themselves upon it, and make themselves, as it were, the equals of their husbands."[9]

The waning status of single dependent women in particular is also suggested by a familiar shift in the use of the word "spinster." Once a positive term for female manufacturers and a reflection of the importance that unmarried women had enjoyed as participants in family industry, "spinster" became, early in the eighteenth century, a term of opprobrium for women beyond the usual age for marriage. By implication, then, dependent women of the middle orders lost status because they ceased to be or to be seen as economic assets to the family and became instead liabilities.[10] This state of things was particularly difficult for women like Fanny Burney, women with aspirations to gentility, for they were prohibited by the definitions of gentility itself from being employed outside the home—at low wages and in occupations already glutted with women from poorer backgrounds—while inside the home fashion, at least, increasingly required them to be idle. More than one father must have advised his daughters, as did Dr. Gregory, to take up needlework that they might have something to occupy their time, for Thomas Gisborne notes that young women in general were unsuccessful in their efforts to "quicken and enliven the slow-paced hours."[11]

All a respectable young woman could really do to ease the

strain of her dependency, and the uneasy status which such dependency entailed, was to marry. But the possibility of marriage in the late eighteenth century, as Daddy Crisp suggests, was becoming increasingly unlikely. Men were marrying late, perhaps because wives were now luxury items, and when men did marry they were liable to require a dowry. Gisborne, in fact, reflects a late eighteenth-century conviction when he suggests that marriage among the middle and upper middle classes was openly becoming a mercantile matter—where a "calculating broker" pored over pedigrees, summed up the property in hand, and computed "at the market price" what a young woman was worth.[12] On top of this, the number of women appears to have exceeded the number of men, all of which must have endorsed the traditionally superior status of single men while it enforced a general lowering of status for single women. For, once young women were of an age for marriage, they were still vulnerable to being seen as liabilities and now as liabilities in overplentiful supply. If, within the family, many single women felt like burdens, the unfavorable conditions of the marriage market must have imposed upon them the even lower identity of merchandise, and it is precisely the discomfort, the oppression of being rendered merchandise, which Burney encounters in *Evelina*, and which she reinvokes as the experience of being assaulted by men.

II

Evelina finds Burney firmly committed to the ideology that marriage is a woman's natural and only destiny and to the understanding that she achieves that destiny by displaying herself and waiting to be chosen. Given Burney's own trauma on the marriage market, this is a commitment which suggests how impoverished any other options must have appeared. Evelina's entrance into the world, like Fanny Burney's, is patently an entry onto the marriage market, and the assemblies, operas, plays, and pleasure gardens, while initiating her into knowledge of society, also function as occasions upon which she is displayed. Indeed, there is some fun early in the novel when Evelina describes the sensation of turning herself out London-style: "You can't think how oddly my head feels; full of powder and black pins, and a great cushion on the top of it" (17). Being an object is odd, but it is also amusing, and it is even thrilling when the princely Lord Orville asks one to dance. But being on display, which is necessary to secure a husband, to fulfill one's destiny, and to be supported, is pleasant only when one is regarded as a fascinating treasure. Unfortunately, the logic of women's economic situation dictates that she may also be regarded as something of lower value—as overstocked merchandise, for example, by men of the lower orders or, at best, by gentlemen as prey.

The workings of this logic are widely, though intuitively, evoked in *Evelina*, for it is women's economic dependency which lurks behind men's easy assumption that Evelina may be pursued, imposed upon, and controlled. Burney, moreover, although she never protests or makes a point of the fact that it *is* a woman's destiny to display herself on the market, is one of the few writers in the century to describe the experience in such a way as to emphasize its discomfort and oppression—and she is one of the very few to take this discomfort seriously. The language of Evelina's response to male assault—she is "provoked," "distressed," "terrified," "angered"—impresses upon us what ought to be obvious—that Evelina finds it oppressive to be raped—and that critics have not noticed this aspect of the novel is merely a comment on what we have come to accept as women's due.[13]

But, while intuitively evoking the discomfort of being forcibly reduced to merchandise or prey, Burney maintains another ideological version of a genteel woman's situation and of her relation to society, a version which is much in conflict with the first. This second version suggests not only that genteel women are not merchandise at all but that there are no shared economic conditions which would tend to impose that identity upon them. And it is this vision of a genteel woman's lot that ameliorates the inescapable experience of being assailed and that ultimately helps establish an eighteenth-century patriarchy, with all its restrictions on young women, as something bearable by and indeed beneficial to young women of the middle classes.

In establishing this vision, Burney simply omits from the novel the economic conditions which in her own life and in the lives of women like her most restricted autonomy and lowered status and which also enforced the authority which men of the middle and landed orders felt in relation to women. Evelina, for example, is a woman of independent fortune, a fact which sets her quite apart from Fanny Burney and probably from the majority of women of good family. Evelina's fortune will not sustain her in a life of fashion, but it may "make her happy, if she is disposed to be so in private life"; and, while hopes of a good marriage are entertained for her by Mr. Villars (her guardian, a character based to some extent on Daddy Crisp), Evelina will never be required to consider a stiff and unremarkable young man for the sake, say, of £3,000 a year (8). But it is not only Evelina who escapes economic restriction. The general economic inequities of men's and women's lives are also omitted from the novel. With the exception of the £30,000 which Evelina's father bestows upon her at the end of the book, we never know, as we do in Austen, how much men and women inherit; we never know how much anyone is worth. And since everyone in the novel appears at leisure, even women and men of the trading classes, we are never in contact with any inequality in access to work.

Indeed, most concern for or consciousness of money is confined to the lower orders, where it is caricatured and dismissed. It is Mr. Smith, for example, a would-be gentleman and the tenant of a silversmith's dining room, who hints most directly at the economic contradiction of men's and women's lots and at the resulting inequities in status and in power. Despite some hapless gestures at courtliness—blunt references to Evelina's beauty and entirely false assertions that he always studies "what the ladies like"—Smith is fond of driving home some distinctly uncourtly realities (171). He is aware that women are economically dependent on men, and he reminds Evelina that "marriage is all in all with the ladies; but with us gentlemen it's quite another thing!" (209). He is also aware that he is a buyer in a buyer's market, and it pleases him to call attention to the fact that the laws of supply and demand make *him* the treasure: ". . . there are a great many other ladies that have been proposed to me . . . so you may very well be proud . . . for I assure you, there is nobody so likely to catch me at last as yourself" (210). The status which male privilege and the conditions of the marriage market confer on Smith provides him in turn with the agreeable conclusion that it is natural, and even desirable, to women that he impose his will on them. Smith, in fact, is "thunderstruck with amazement" when Evelina refuses the assembly tickets he has tried to force upon her, and with the self-righteousness of one who feels that society has empowered *him* to do the imposing he "thought proper to desire [she] would tell him [her] reasons" (164).

Young Branghton, Evelina's cousin and the son and heir of a silversmith, has even fewer pretensions to courtliness than Mr. Smith; he merely assumes, with some candor, that those who can confer economic benefits have a right to dictate. He is eager, therefore, to pay for Evelina's coach fares and opera tickets and to treat her at public places, for "if I pay, I think I've a right to have it my own way" (172). Like Mr. Smith, young Branghton is highly conscious of the fact that women depend on men and marriage, and like Smith he is fond of twitting them about their inability to impose their will on men. Indeed, his entire relation with his sisters consists of tormenting them about their lack of marriageable qualities.

They will never get a man because they are "ugly enough to frighten a horse" and liable to being exposed with "all their dirty things on, and all their hair about their ears" (160).

Consciousness of money, of its relation to men's superior status and to their control over women, is made so rude and so untenable in Branghton and Smith that it may easily be mocked. But, more than that, in Branghton and Smith the very existence of this consciousness is explained away. It is not a response, not even an exaggerated response, to economic realities but merely a habit of mind apt to be cultivated by persons among the lower orders and particularly by persons in trade. Branghton, especially, is seen as reflecting an obsessive interest in money and prices, profit and advance, weights and measures, and physical qualities in general. In this context any attention to money in its relation to women, status, and power may be put down as one more vulgarity of the lower orders, may be cast with other perversities, like references to untidy hair and dirty underclothes, may be laughed off the stage. In the guise, then, of satirizing the vulgarities of station, Burney undermines an economic consciousness which was not at all confined to the trading classes and which was, in fact, generally imposed by real economic conditions on genteel young women like herself. In the process she also mystifies the reality of the economic conditions which were sustained by a landed patriarchy as a whole and especially by men of the ruling class.

What Burney also mystifies is community—community as the locus of shared and demeaning attitudes toward women. Although almost all men in the novel are unified in their readiness to see women as merchandise or prey, we do not feel the weight of their shared attitudes as we do in, say, *Pride and Prejudice*. For one thing, Evelina, unlike Elizabeth Bennet, is distinctly a tourist, not a fixed member of a community, and we feel that she will not be in contact with these demeaning attitudes long enough to be damaged by them. And, since the community itself is most often represented by a series of ever changing social gatherings, it appears atomistic rather than organic. The same individuals may be thrown repeatedly into one another's company, but we have little sense of their *living* together, of their acting in accord for good or ill. Intuitively and defensively, Burney provides Evelina with a community essentially lacking in communal power and thereby protects her from the concerted socializing forces with which she herself was familiar.

In effect, Burney siphons off what must have seemed to her most restrictive and objectionable in a patriarchal order and either omits or confines it safely to the trading classes. These are deft although not conscious maneuvers, but they leave a certain vacuum in the history of her heroine. For if it is not a woman's economic lot and if it is not demeaning communal attitudes toward women which account for the ease with which tradesmen and gentlemen impose themselves upon Evelina, what then is it? We are left with a chronicle of assorted violations and abuses which have no overt or systematic rationale in the world of this novel.

III

There are several ways in which Burney's historical situation may have prompted her to veil the causal relation between women's economic dependency and their subjection to male control. The 1770s, for example, were not characterized by the rampant awareness of money that was to come with early industrial capitalism,[14] and this in itself may have allowed Burney a certain ease in omitting the facts of women's economic situation from her novel and in condemning economic consciousness itself by ensconcing it amid the vulgarities of the lower orders. But, most important, Burney's historical situation also offered her a reconciling ideology about genteel women. By crediting and giving value to the view that women of good family are really treasure rather than merchandise, *Evelina* reflects a renewed and widespread tendency in the late eighteenth century, especially in its literature, to idealize women of the genteel classes.

In emphasizing male violation and control, moreover, *Evelina* reflects a related cultural and literary preoccupation: the interesting habit of seeing idealized women as persons being pursued by morally inferior males. "The drama of the aggressive male checked by the virtuous woman" has been variously interpreted.[15] But in the work of female writers like Fanny Burney the drama has been seen as an expression of the fact that women really did feel controlled and imposed upon by men and as an expression of the fact that they were prompted to counter this disturbing awareness with an adherence to some mitigating fiction or ideology.[16] What we also find in Burney, however, is evidence that awareness of male oppression did not necessarily go hand in hand with objection to a patriarchal order. *Evelina,* in fact, actually celebrates the rule of landed men by implying that only ruling-class men (never women themselves) have the power to give courtly fiction the potency of ideology, have the ability, in other words, to make the equation of women and treasure seem *real.*

There is some logic, moreover, to this association, for courtly ideologies about women have traditionally been connected with landed males.[17] They are the kinds of fiction which very powerful men have been able to afford in relation to women. In the late eighteenth century, moreover, the power of the male gentry would have been great enough to give courtliness-as-ideology some general currency, and Burney, with her family connections to the great, must have been immersed in the beliefs which ruling-class males entertained about themselves and their relations to others. In *Evelina,* at least, it is Burney's association of courtly fiction, the idealization of genteel women, with men of the ruling class that finally permits her to endorse male control, a patriarchal system in general, and the rule of landed men and to make all three seem endurable to women.

In addition, of course, it would have been futile in 1778 for someone like Burney to protest against the rule of landed men or the lot of genteel women—and, more than anything else perhaps, this lack of option and this sense of almost total male ruling-class authority make Burney the last major female writer to give credit to the courtly fictions of landed men. But, even for Burney, to endorse patriarchy, to endorse the authority of ruling-class men, is to be immersed in tension and in contradiction. One contradiction, for example, is the fact that Burney endorses the authority of landed men while demonstrating that the superior authority of the male gentry is most dramatically revealed in their ability to control and oppress women with greater success than do men of the lower orders—for it is ruling-class men who have the greatest facility in insulting Evelina on the streets, entrapping her in their carriages, and laying hands upon her in public places.

The superior control of ruling-class men is seen most pointedly in the ballroom. The rules of the dance, of course, which express social order in general, confirm all men's authority as choosers. But the lowly Mr. Smith is less adroit and less forceful than Lovel or Sir Clement in making use of his authority. *His* attempts to foist himself as a partner upon Evelina are deftly foiled by Evelina herself, with the result that Smith is forced to dance with Evelina's grandmother, Madame Duval. When Smith, "being extremely chagrined," complains of Evelina's refusal, she responds with a "total disregard" which "made him soon change the subject" (209). Lovel, in contrast—he is a fop but still a gentleman—does not take so lightly to being deprived of authority and status. When Evelina innocently refuses him and then accepts Lord Orville, Lovel becomes indignant, abuses Evelina until she is "ready to die with shame," and then persecutes her for the rest of the novel (22).

Still, if men of the gentry are more effective at assault than men of the lower orders, their assaults on Evelina are, for

Burney at least, easier to take. For, even in behavior, men of the ruling class imply not that Evelina is merchandise but, rather, that she is sexual prey. The distinction now may seem nonexistent, but evidently for Burney it is less invidious that Evelina be identified as Eve than that she be identified as goods, and the contempt expressed for Mr. Smith is far stronger than the disapproval directed at Lord Merton, the most openly licentious of the ruling-class males. There is reason, too, for this disparity in judgment if one considers that the first identity—sexual prey—was not only more traditional but less liable to being supported by members of one's family. Evelina and Fanny know that they are chaste, that they are not easy prey, and no one close to them could think otherwise. The second identity, however—marketable goods—is one which the economic conditions of the age had already threatened to impose on Burney and one which her family seemed inclined to endorse. When confronted with two insulting versions of a genteel woman's status, Burney instinctively and naturally focuses upon the version least likely to be given credit by family or friends.

The greatest distinction, however, between the oppressive control of ruling-class men and that of lower-class men is that the former is more evenly and more consistently overlaid with courtly fiction. The behavior of the male gentry may imply that Evelina is really Eve, but their language sustains the fiction that she is Cinderella. Lord Merton, for example, feels doubly legitimized as a ruling-class male to force his attentions on Evelina. It is his "conscious quality" which prompts his "look of libertinism" toward women in general and the bold eyes, "rude questions and free compliments" which he directs at Evelina (102, 258). But as a member of the gentry Lord Merton has also tuned his gallantries to the highest pitch. He may behave as if Evelina were prey, but his "fine speeches and compliments" make her think herself a "goddess" and Lord Merton "a pagan, paying [her] adoration" (100).

The epitome of this split between sexual assault and courtly devotion is found in Sir Clement Willoughby, a character about whom both Evelina and her creator make some paradoxical judgments. When Sir Clement rescues Evelina at Vauxhall, when he rescues her from one set of tormentors so he may prey upon her himself, he reveals that Evelina is Eve to him too. Despite his past experience of her innocence, he ignores the information that she has lost her companions and assumes that her presence in the garden is a sign of her sexual availability. This is the basis upon which most ruling-class men are ready to deal with her: despite all protestations to the effect that she is Cinderella, the fascinating treasure, the beautiful but distant object, their behavior implies that she is both prey and willing prey.

What distinguishes Sir Clement from Lord Merton, however, is the persistence with which he imposes upon his control of Evelina the courtly fiction that she *is* Cinderella. At their first encounter, for example, Sir Clement's courtly language marks a farcical counterpoint to his behavior. As he pursues Evelina about the ballroom, badgering her with questions about the dance partner whom she has invented to avoid him, imposing his presence over her protest, and ultimately forcing her to dance, he sustains a running and sometimes hilarious pose as the powerless lover of an unreachable mistress: ". . . it cannot be that you are so cruel! Softness itself is painted in your eyes:—You could not, surely, have the barbarity so wantonly to trifle with my misery?" (30). This is stuff and even Evelina knows it.

Once Sir Clement has fixed upon her as his sexual prey, he employs the same courtly fiction with greater earnestness to disguise his seductive intentions and to manipulate Evelina's response. Evelina, at these moments, is usually too agitated to reflect, but Burney herself maintains a clear distinction between what is truth and what is story. When Sir Clement is most in control, when he is imposing himself most forcibly, he is, ludicrously enough, the most devoted lover. After the opera, for example, having kidnapped Evelina in his carriage, having directed the driver into the London night, and having so terrified her that she is prompted to leap from the chariot door, Sir Clement seizes her and assures her that "my life is at your devotion" (87). When Evelina strains this fiction by thrusting her head from the window and calling for aid, Sir Clement simply retreats into his role and for the moment becomes convincing as the humble lover: "Sir Clement now poured forth abundant protestations of honour, and assurances of respect, entreating my pardon for having offended me, and beseeching my good opinion" (88).

It should be evident, I think, that Sir Clement has the honor of a rapist, perhaps a rapist *manqué*, and Burney seems conscious of this when she has Mr. Villars condemn him: "Sir Clement, though he seeks occasion to give real offence, contrives to avoid all appearance of intentional evil" (104). Evelina, too, is allowed to turn from much of his "nonsense" with "real disgust" (30). And yet she is permitted to forgive him, usually in the same scene and always in response to his pose as courtly lover. Here is Evelina after her first kidnapping: ". . . he flung himself on his knees, and pleaded with so much submission, that I was really obliged to forgive him, because his humiliation made me quite ashamed" (88). And here is Evelina after her second: ". . . indeed, I knew not how to resist the humility of his intreaties" (184). In her more rational moments, moreover, Evelina is allowed to prefer Sir Clement to the hapless Mr. Smith, the would-be lover whose assaults upon her are far less persistent than Sir Clement's and, from one point of view at least, less reprehensible: "It is true, no man can possibly pay me greater compliments, or make more fine speeches, than Sir Clement Willoughby: yet his language, though too flowery, is always that of a gentleman; and his address and manners are so very superior . . . that, to make any comparison between him and Mr. Smith would be extremely unjust" (163).

What has been pilloried here as snobbishness—and Evelina *is* a snob, with Burney's approval—must also be seen as a positive response to Sir Clement's courtly fictions, a response in which Burney shares. For, despite the flimsiness of fictions like these, they may still be valued and indeed have been valued throughout history. Given the all but absolute authority of ruling-class men, given economic and social conditions which one could not alter and which tended to impose the identity of merchandise or prey, given the lack of options to marriage and the marriage market, in particular, it was perhaps all one could do to sustain, intuitively and unthinkingly, the ideologies which gave support to one's sense of value. Mr. Smith offends because he both violates Evelina's will and flaunts the social and economic context which licenses him to do so. He reminds Evelina, in other words, of the real and overpowering forces at work. Fiction is sometimes preferable to truths like these, especially when it occasionally seems to be the truth, as is the case with the apologies of Sir Clement.

What Burney unconsciously reveals, then, in Evelina's ambivalence toward Sir Clement and in her own, is that the situation of a genteel unmarried woman could force her to credit and give value to ideologies about her experience which at some level she understood to be untrue. Indeed, Burney's main response to the essentially oppressive nature of Evelina's experience and her own, her main response to what she admits about male control in Sir Clement, is to create a greater and more courtly fiction yet—and that fiction, of course, is Lord Orville. This elegant and truly polite young man of noble birth and handsome fortune, who takes upon himself the rigors of uninterrupted noblesse oblige and courtliness, is meant to represent landed patriarchy not only as it should be but as Burney wishes to believe it is. The fiction of Lord Orville, who has all the vapid perfection of wish fulfillment, is that he reverses the normal relation between male privilege and male control. While almost every other man in the novel finds in his economic and social privilege a justification for imposing his will upon others, and in particular upon women, Lord Orville, the most privileged man in the novel, converts every social and economic benefit into a motive for deferring to or reaffirming the autonomy and status of others:

> Far from being indolently satisfied with his own accomplishments, as I have already observed many men here are, though without any pretensions to his merit, he is most assiduously attentive to please and to serve all who are in his company; and, though his success is invariable, he never manifests the smallest degree of consciousness. (61)

Lord Orville's particular value as wish fulfillment is that he confers the identity of treasure upon Evelina—not just in language but in behavior too. At the first assembly, for example, when Evelina is most at loose ends, able neither to speak nor to act as she desires and behaving least like a woman of gentility and polish, Lord Orville gently encourages her to express her will and behaves in general as if she were a person of equal if not superior status: ". . . had I been the person of the most consequence in the room, I could not have met with more attention and respect" (21). This affirmation of her status as treasure is most thoroughly realized in Lord Orville's courtship of Evelina, for this princely young man ignores all the usual requirements of marriage by proposing to a young woman of obscure parentage and slender means, thus permanently conferring upon her the identity of Cinderella. The wish fulfillment is so perfect and so complete that Burney is moved, rather uneasily, I think, to reassure us that the hero has not been parted from his senses:

> When I expressed my amazement that he could honour with his choice a girl who seemed so infinitely, in *every* respect, beneath his alliance, he frankly owned, that he had fully intended making more minute inquiries into my family and connections, . . . but the suddenness of my intended journey,

> and the uncertainty of seeing me again, put him quite off his guard, and "divesting him of prudence, left him nothing but love." (371)

Lord Orville is indeed too good to be true, and like all Prince Charmings, I suspect, his extraordinary virtues are not only compensation but justification for the way things are. For it should be clear that the consistent courtliness of Lord Orville tends to justify ruling-class male control and that Lord Orville, as an exemplum of what male authority ought to be, of what Burney wishes to believe it is, provides a counterweight to persons like Sir Clement, whose courtly fictions barely conceal what a landed patriarchal order, in its abuse of women, really felt like.

The remorse of Sir John Belmont, Evelina's real father, is a further endorsement of the landed and patriarchal order, for in contrast to men of the trading classes, who are evidently incapable of reform, Sir John demonstrates at length the inclination and capacity of ruling-class men to take upon themselves the sole responsibility for justice and their own redemption. Having long since recognized the real status of his wife, Caroline—she is not prey but treasure—Sir John ritually humiliates himself in front of Evelina, the "dear resemblance of [her] murdered mother": ". . . behold thy father at thy feet!—bending thus lowly to implore you would not hate him" (367, 368). What is more, Sir John is prepared to share with Evelina the benefits of his social and economic privilege. She is to have birth *and* fortune—an immediate £30,000 and an extra £1,000 "which he insisted that I should receive entirely for my own use, and expend in equipping myself properly for the new rank of life to which I seem destined" (372). Here is another benefit of supporting the landed patriarchy.

There is undeniable zest on Burney's part over Evelina's acquisition of birth and fortune, and her zest is particularly evident because this is the only time in the novel that we know what anyone is worth. But Burney's enthusiasm for Evelina's rise is carefully controlled in the interests of tradition, for as an author she shares little of Austen's or of Richardson's delight in merging the ruling class with persons of the lower orders. It is significant, for example, that Burney tells us only what is bestowed on Evelina by her father and that this rightful fortune, the fortune to which she has been born, is bestowed before her marriage to Lord Orville. The effect is to undermine any emphasis on profit in Evelina's marriage and to guard against any real challenge to the integrity of class divisions. Lord Orville is allowed to find treasure in a woman of small fortune, but that woman is then established as an heiress and the daughter of a baronet. Ultimately, the love plot in this novel represents no dilution of the ruling orders, and, despite Evelina's rise, oligarchy, patriarchy, and the status quo are triumphant. Burney's endorsement of class divisions goes hand in hand with her ultimate endorsement of women's subordination to men.

IV

But *Evelina*, of course, is more than a simple endorsement of patriarchy—as run by gentlemen—and of the ideologies with which it justifies and mitigates its power. It is also the history of a young woman's progress, a form of Erbildungsroman. It is possible to see in Evelina's progress, for example, some reflections of a traditional male quest plot or initiation story. Like many a young man, Evelina enters the world, is initiated into the nature of her society, and, one might argue, grows in prudence and good judgment. For the first two volumes of the novel, in fact, she satirizes male conceit, resists male control, and becomes increasingly skillful at exerting what in this novel is a highly significant form of power —the power of self-defense, a form of power as autonomy. To a limited degree, in fact, *Evelina* entertains a fantasy of female power which is in some tension with the novel's endorsement and idealization of landed male control. The nature of that autonomy is subtle and it is also deliberately qualified, for Burney feared above all things "ridicule or censure as a female."[18] But, as George Eliot has put it, "yoked creatures" may have their "private opinions,"[19] and it is Evelina's private opinions which are the source of what we must call her power in this novel.

Evelina is capable of private opinions because of her extraordinary innocence and inexperience, traditionally feminine qualities which tend to excuse those opinions at the same time that they provide their source. In the myth of Evelina's childhood, she has grown up "naturally" at Berry Hill and has been nurtured in this complete rural isolation by a foster father who is a clergyman and an isolate, a man totally uncorrupted by the privileges of sex and rank. Thus when Evelina enters the world—as represented by London, Bristol, and Howard Grove—she enters with a perfectly unjaundiced eye and an unsullied if modest sense of her own consequence. One form of autonomy which this feminine innocence allows her is the power to resist the humiliating visions of herself which the male community is ready to impose. It is Evelina's private opinion that she is neither merchandise nor prey, and it is primarily her early protection from these distorting notions which assures us that her homegrown consequence will never be impaired.

Evelina's inexperience is also the source of her private opinions about the community itself, for she is the traditional innocent, unused to the manners of the great world and therefore able to observe them from the perspective of what is "natural and right." Since most of her letters in the first two volumes are composed of satiric observations and critical judgments about the presumption and the assaults of men, it is evidently *not* natural or right, from Evelina's point of view, that men should assume superiority to or control over women. Here, for example, is her response to her first assembly: "The gentlemen, as they passed and repassed, looked as if they thought we were quite at their disposal, and only waiting for the honour of their commands; . . . and I thought it so provoking, that I determined in my own mind that, far from humouring such airs, I would rather not dance at all" (17, 18). Satire, it should be noted, is one form of autonomy, and Evelina is a nimble satirist of the presumption and conceit of males.

But Evelina does more than satirize. In her inexperience, she also *acts*—rashly and rebelliously—which is another degree of autonomy altogether. She refuses Lovel, accepts Lord Orville, laughs out loud when Lovel complains, criticizes Sir Clement, and tries to elude him, all because she feels like it, because her natural self-consequence prompts her to act in direct contradiction to the rules of behavior which give men the authority to choose—and the rationale for feeling arrogant—and which give women the right politely to refuse and then only if they are willing to forgo the pleasures of dancing altogether. It is this turn for satire and this impulse to resist which make Evelina powerful and refreshing: she is feminine but not, initially at least, completely passive, and in the guise of innocent response she musters no little resistance to the oppressions and assaults of patriarchy.

Evelina's modest power, however, is in tension with Burney's justification of male ruling-class control and with the ideology that genteel women are really treasure, and this tension is suggested in a variety of defensive strategies, ranging from assurances of Evelina's innocence to qualifications of her autonomy and ultimately to the abandonment of the quest plot altogether. One strategy which prevents the conventional reader from taking umbrage, from leveling censure at Evelina "as a female," is Burney's emphasis upon that innocence and inexperience which prompt Evelina to be satirical and to rebel in the first place. Although we are invited to agree with Evelina as a critical observer, we are also invited to regard her with a fairly patronizing air. She is still a "little rustic," a perceptive little rustic to be sure, but for all her wit she is still a charming, because innocent, country girl (9). Evelina also confines her satire to letters meant only for her guardian—much as the "silent observant Miss Fanny" confined her satiric strictures to her diary or to correspondence with her sisters and with Daddy Crisp.[20] There can be little protest, after all, about a yoked creature having her own opinions if those opinions are not allowed to circulate freely. Letter writing, as a narrative mode, functions in *Evelina* in a traditionally feminine way: it passes off public criticism as private and therefore innocent remark. Evelina's impulsive actions, however, her breaking of the rules, are quite another thing. They may be satisfying to the reader, but they are officially incorrect, and the nearer they come to being deliberate the more they are criticized. Mr. Villars, for example, forgives Evelina for ignorantly refusing one partner and then accepting another but not for making up a partner to escape Sir Clement: "I am sure I need not say, how much more I was pleased with the mistakes of your inexperience at the private ball, than with the attempted adoption of more fashionable manners at the ridotto. But your confusion and mortifications were such as to entirely silence all reproofs on my part" (44).

Mr. Villars lays a finger here on still another way in which Burney qualifies, and therefore secures toleration for, Evelina's autonomy. Evelina's impulsive resistance to restriction gets her into trouble, succeeds in making *her* feel mortification. Her autonomy in one quarter, moreover, is continually juxtaposed with an ostensibly charming failure of self-control in another. For, if Evelina makes some efforts at self-assertion with Lovel and Sir Clement, she can barely speak to Lord Orville, so awed is she by his superior "manners," "figure," and "rank." It is simply impossible to censure her for being too bold when the kindly attentions of a lord reduce her to hanging her head, looking at her fan, and feeling a fool.

As if this were not enough, Evelina is also made ineffective in asserting herself with gentlemen, even with Lovel, and her ineffectiveness in turn opens the way for male protection. Lord Orville intervenes for her "with some warmth" when Lovel demands an explanation, leads Sir Clement away from her after she has burst into tears, risks a duel to insure her against Lovel's insults in the future, and is given to offering his coach, inquiring after her safety, and expressing general concern for her well-being. These encounters with Lord Orville keep us in touch with the notion that, however charmingly satiric, Evelina still needs someone to protect her, and this is a view of Burney's heroine which is confirmed by the very structure of the novel, for Evelina's narrative letters are regularly interspersed with replies from Mr. Villars. The latter, by always correcting or affirming Evelina's judgments, commending or gently censuring her behavior, reminds us all the while that she is a young woman merely on leave from fatherly supervision and paternal protection.

V

Still, for all the qualification of her powers, Evelina does grow in autonomy and self-control, not with gentlemen, to be sure, but with men of the trading and aspiring classes. Mr. Smith may force her to attend the Hampstead assembly, but he cannot make her dance, for Evelina has learned the rules, and she has also acquired some spirit to use them for her own protection: ". . . the extreme vanity of this man, makes me exert a spirit which I did not, till now, know that I possessed" (210). Eventually she manages such "reserve and coldness" that both Smith and Branghton are persuaded to leave her alone (228).

The quest plot of this novel, which is partially realized in Evelina's success at finally defending herself against the two men most inclined to see her as merchandise, may be seen as a projection of Burney's vague hankerings for revenge, revenge not on the trading classes, for the view of women as merchandise was not confined in life to the lower orders, but revenge—unthinkingly, confusedly—on the disparaging attitudes toward single women that were much more widely spread. It was unthinkable perhaps for Burney to oppose herself to what actually sustained those attitudes in life: the landed patriarchal order as a whole and specifically the economic contradiction between genteel men and women. It was equally impossible perhaps even to locate the patriarchal order as the source of women's lowered status. Evelina's victory, therefore, is the working out of anger and of a desire for revenge, but of revenge in a sphere where revenge was safe, where it could even be approved of by those with real authority—and Burney's upper-class readers were especially fond of her satires on the vulgarity of the trading orders.

It is also evident from the ease of Evelina's victory that Burney considered the trading orders an easy mark, for in 1778 industrial takeoff, along with the dramatic rise of men in trade, had not yet begun. Men of the trading classes, therefore, may be bested by a woman, while gentlemen cannot because, from Burney's point of view, the former lack social and political consequence. Their awareness of money and of money's relation to status and power may be scorned because there is no conscious danger of its becoming more widespread. And the mercantile vision of women, which they are made to represent, may be summarily dismissed because, in one so committed to courtly ideologies and to males of the ruling class, that vision could not be conceived of as the coming thing.

Evelina, then, is allowed a limited victory with Branghton and Smith, but that is all, for the whole notion of her progress in autonomy and self-defense is in conflict with Burney's idealization of male control, with the courtly fiction that she wishes to sustain, and with the "happy ending" that she must create to secure that fiction for her heroine. The conditions of quest are in conflict with the requirements of marriage and of love. Evelina therefore may acquire a certain skill in fending off assault—no mean accomplishment in this novel—but her responsibility as an adult is not to maintain that ability. Quite the opposite: her destiny is to *be* protected, that is, to marry, and her preparation for this future must be to abdicate rather than to maintain her power. In the third volume, therefore, Evelina moves from the ranks of the trading classes and from the vulgar household of Madame Duval to the upper-class establishment of Mrs. Beaumont, where she feels so ill at ease among her social superiors that she loses all her previous "spirit" and responds to the most flagrant forms of abuse with blushes and silence.

The third volume also marks a shift in the locus of satiric observation. In the first two volumes Evelina is almost alone as a satiric observer, and her eye for the ridiculous makes us feel, despite her ineffectiveness in action and her deference to Lord Orville, that she is still a person of some autonomy and self-control. In the third volume, however, by far the greater share of satirical observation belongs to Mrs. Selwyn, a woman who is witty, effective, and appealing but who is also roundly condemned. Mr. Villars has "often been disgusted at her unmerciful propensity to satire" (254). Sir Clement censures her for the "unbounded license of her tongue"—a quality "intolerable" in a woman—and Evelina, who is surprised at Mrs. Selwyn's "severity," observes that she is both "*masculine*" and wanting in "gentleness" (325, 256, 254). That Mrs. Selwyn is still undeniably attractive to the reader is a measure perhaps of Burney's own ambivalence, for love of the ridiculous was her best quality as a writer; but, whatever its value in a novelist, a turn for satire was hardly a virtue in a bride.

To deprive Evelina of satire, of course, is to deprive her of power. But, since abdication of power is a traditional preparation for marriage, Burney, despite her inner conflicts, continues officially to endorse the status quo. What one senses, then, in the condemnation of Mrs. Selwyn is a preparation for matrimony, an attempt to mitigate our sense that Evelina has been powerful, because satirical, in the first two volumes of the novel. Indeed, the Evelina of the third volume is characterized less by satire than by sentiment, and the imprudent but lively reactions of the first and second volumes give way to the more traditionally sanctioned activities, like the weeping and fainting, of the third. Evelina's discovery of her brother, Mr. Macartney, and her reconciliation with her father provide grand occasions for the display of sentiment while reaffirming the value of family, of family feeling, and in particular of filial affection: Evelina spends a good part of the scene with Belmont at her father's feet and upon her knees.

The end of *Evelina*, then, is marked by a decline in Evelina's autonomy, an autonomy which is in tension not just with matrimony but with landed patriarchy as a whole. The novel's quest plot is dissolved into its love plot, and Evelina must marry. Ideologically, in literature and in life, there is no other "happy ending." Evelina's progress in self-defense must be cut short. Her "progress," in fact, is circular, for her encounter with the world is finally a genteel woman's traditional encounter; it is a time of waiting, a time of transition, during which she is transferred from the protection of one male authority to the protection of another. The entire action of *Evelina* in fact takes place on an extended leave from one guardian and culminates in the acquisition of another, whose nuptial promise is that he will protect her: ". . . then shall it be the sole study of my life to endeavour to soften your past,—and guard you from future misfortunes!" (350). Lord Orville is also closely identified in character with Evelina's guardian. In volume 1 we are told that Orville's "sweetness, politeness, and diffidence" will ripen into Villars' "benevolence, dignity, and goodness" (61). And in volume 3 Evelina exclaims: ". . . was there ever such another man as Lord Orville?—Yes, *one* other now resides at Berry

Hill!" (302). Lord Orville and Reverend Villars: even the names are similar, and at the end of the novel Evelina and Orville return to Villars and to Berry Hill. It is a fitting locus for the end of a journey which has taken her from protected minor to *femme couverte*.

VI

Since Evelina is not responsible for her future, since her destiny is to be protected from rather than to act upon the world, to receive the identity of treasure rather than to create it, we cannot attach to her growth and autonomy the same significance we might attach to the growth and autonomy of a young man. However much we value her wit and rebellious behavior, we must value male authority even more, and Burney, perhaps in compensation for her heroine's decline, devotes much of the last volume to a demonstration of the fact that female power is not enough. Evelina, we will remember, has been reduced to silence and blushes by the affronts of Mrs. Beaumont's guests, when Lord Orville begins to intervene, with increasing frequency, on her behalf. As he continues to intervene, he acquires a series of titles which justify him in the role of protector. In the first two volumes he bears little more than the title of a dance partner, but in the third he moves quickly from friend to brother to lover and ultimately to husband. Each title lends him increasing authority to protect Evelina from the lascivious energies of Lord Merton and Sir Clement.

But the culmination of Lord Orville's intervention and of the novel's justification of ruling-class male control comes in the last episode, in Lord Orville's encounter with Captain Mirvan, who is the ultimate expression of that authority or power to impose oneself which society has fostered in males, especially males of the ruling class. The captain would appear to be the younger son of a country gentleman, the untutored sort for whom a naval commission might be purchased but the sort who remained rude and countrified, although he might marry the daughter of a lady (Mrs. Mirvan is the daughter of Lady Howard). The captain may also represent an earlier and rougher version of the ruling-class male, for Madame Duval calls his rudeness old-fashioned and Mirvan, in contrast to all the younger gentry in the novel, makes no stab whatsoever at seeming courtly. Whatever his heritage, however, Captain Mirvan embodies the most open and most physically brutal expression of male control in the novel, and he is the one man in relation to whom all women are consistently without resources.

Most men in the book impose themselves on women only, whereas Mirvan imposes himself on the world. But his attacks on "unmanly men" suggest that the essence of "manly" power is to him control over women and that men ought to make this control explicit, not disguise or soften it with fictions. Courtliness, from the captain's point of view, is degrading to men and women both: ". . . the men, as they call themselves, are no better than monkeys; and as to the women, why they are mere dolls" (101). To be a real man is to exert force without concealment, and Mirvan as a real man, husband, and father relishes the control he can impose on any woman even vaguely connected with him: ". . . I never suffer anybody to be in a passion in my house, but myself"; ". . . I expect obedience and submission to orders"; "I charge you . . . that you'll never again be so impertinent as to have a taste of your own before my face" (174, 124, 98).

The captain's assaults on Madame Duval, the most physically brutal in the novel, combine two aspects of the landed patriarchy for which he stands—the force which men, especially men of the ruling class, feel authorized to use against women and the force employed by the state, and its feudal representatives, against traditional enemies: the captain first attacks Duval for being French and then pursues his torments, it would appear, because she is a nonsubmissive woman. As a representative of the landed patriarchy, then,

Captain Mirvan suggests the mutually reenforcing relation between the control belonging to the head of state, to the paterfamilias, and to the male civilian; and in his brutality he represents the capacity for physical violence which underlies and enforces the control of all three. When verbal insult is insufficient to his feelings, the captain simply attacks Duval physically, seizes her wrists, threatens to throw her from windows, pushes her into puddles, shakes her until she sobs, and ultimately, under cover of a fake robbery, drags her down a road, throws her into a ditch, and ties her to a tree. He is an image of the violence potential in patriarchy, even patriarchy in the hands of gentlemen, and as such he suggests the real necessity for reconciliation to the patriarchal order.

Women in the novel, accordingly, appear almost totally powerless to oppose Mirvan's show of force. Mrs. Mirvan, who at least tries to dissuade Sir Clement when he is pursuing Evelina, does not dare speak to the captain when he is out of humor and attempts little more than distracting him from brutalities when he is in. Maria Mirvan is merely a shadow and suffers in silence while her father makes "rude jests upon the bad shape of her nose" (27). Lady Howard has a "sort of tacit agreement . . . that she should not appear to be acquainted with his schemes" (127). And that the untitled captain disrupts the peace of courtly Howard Grove is a classic example of the extent to which gender outranks class position—even Evelina is intimidated into silence when the captain plays his most brutal tricks on her grandmother, Madame Duval. Burney, moreover, far from disapproving this feminine meekness, appears to endorse and support it, for Madame Duval, the one woman who tries to resist the captain's control, becomes herself an object of satire by abusing the captain's "ill-politeness" in terms which are themselves a study in rudeness and vulgarity. Both the tone and the fact of her resistance are also explained away by her origins. She began life as a "waiting-girl" in a tavern, married above her station, acquired wealth and pretensions to gentility, but remained "uneducated and unprincipled; ungentle in her temper, and unamiable in her manners" (3). Her recalcitrance, therefore, is nothing the novel endorses: only a lower-class woman would meet force with force.

What is more, Duval's assertions of herself against the captain are also ineffective, for he is always the more powerful antagonist. The captain's attacks upon Duval leave her screaming for help, sobbing with passion, crying in pain, and roaring "in the utmost agony of rage and terror" (133). So much for women who resist. None of the other women, either, ever come to her assistance. Lady Howard pretends not to know what is afoot. Evelina is afraid to tell her that the robbery is a fake, and Mrs. Mirvan politely despairs of having any influence whatsoever on her husband's conduct. Bonding between women, it would seem, is futile, and it is finally Sir Clement who, at Evelina's request, puts a momentary end to the captain's brutalities by leaving for London.

The captain then disappears for some 250 pages, but when he is brought back on stage, in the last episode of the novel, he is brought back to demonstrate once again the violence and the force of bad male energies, with the understanding of course that the bad male energies which count are those of gentlemen. Mirvan is also brought back to demonstrate the powerlessness of females, for this is finally what justifies male control in *Evelina*. Real power in this novel, one should note, is actually defined so as to preclude women generally from having their share, for power in *Evelina* is the power of control, the power to impose oneself forcibly upon another or to defend oneself against being forcibly imposed upon. This is not the kind of power which women have ever had much authority or opportunity to use. It is, however, the kind of power which landed men really enjoyed not just in relation to women but in relation to most men who were not of the ruling class, and these landed men supply the model of power in *Evelina*.

It is this power of control and of defense against it which

Mirvan and Orville display in the last episode of the novel. The captain has imposed himself upon the company by dressing up a monkey and introducing it as Lovel's relation. The monkey is biting Lovel's ear rather painfully; the captain is laughing; and the frightened ladies are jumping upon their chairs when Lord Orville, "ever humane, generous, and benevolent," flings the monkey from the room and shuts the door (383). This is Orville's most decisive action in the book —the only time anyone succeeds in containing Mirvan— and what it tells us, once and for all, is something the novel has already taught us: that only good and ruling-class male control is effective against bad, that women's power in particular is not effectual, that female abdication of autonomy is therefore justified, and that in a world demonstrably full of bad male energies the only lasting protection is to marry.

2. *Pride and Prejudice*

One feels at once in *Pride and Prejudice* something entirely foreign to *Evelina*, an edge, a critical emphasis given to the economic contradiction of men's and women's lives. The details of this contradiction are as carefully recorded in *Pride and Prejudice* as they are carefully omitted in *Evelina*, and the economic disparity between the lives of women and of men receives major emphasis in the situation of Austen's heroine. Elizabeth Bennet, in contrast to Evelina, has no decent fortune whatsoever. She *must* marry; she must marry with an eye to money; and the reason she must marry is that the family inheritance has been settled on a male. It would be hard to make more central point of the fact that the conditions of economic life favored men and restricted women.

The entailed fortune which so obviously benefits Mr. Collins and so obviously restricts Jane Austen's heroine is merely the epitome of an economic privilege that is granted men in general and of an economic restriction that is imposed on women, and the details of that privilege and restriction are explicitly recorded throughout the novel. It is the right of Austen's men to have work that pays and to rise through preference and education, and we are directly told, as we are never told in Burney, who has had access to what. We are told that Mr. Gardiner and Mr. Philips are established in business and in law, that Sir William Lucas has retired from trade, that Collins has been sent to the university and granted a living, and that Wickham has been set up first as clergyman, then as lawyer, and finally as officer—prospects which he persistently rejects or squanders. But men, no matter how hapless and undeserving, must be provided for, must be given every opportunity to earn their way.

Women, in contrast, are prepared for nothing but display. Their goal is not to accomplish but to be "accomplished" or, as Miss Bingley puts it, to be "esteemed accomplished."[1] And Austen does not fail to tell us what "accomplished" means—being able to paint tables, net purses, and cover screens. Women have no access at all to work that pays, for in this novel, in contrast, say, to *Emma*, even the life of a governess is not an option. (The governesses of *Pride and Prejudice* are not a promising lot. Mrs. Annesley may be "well-bred," but Mrs. Jenkinson has been extinguished as a personality, and the immoral Mrs. Younge has been reduced to letting rooms and taking bribes.) Finally, although women and men both inherit money, women inherit a lump sum, a kind of dowry, while men inherit livings, and Austen tells us precisely who has inherited what. The Miss Bingleys are worth £20,000 while their brother has an annual four or five. Miss Darcy's fortune is £30,000, her brother's £10,000 per annum. And Mrs. Bennet has a total of £4,000 while her husband nets £2,000 a year.

The first two sentences of the novel make subtle and ironic point of this disparity, and they evoke the way in which economic inequity shapes male and female power:

> It is a truth universally acknowledged, that a single man in possession of a good fortune must be in want of a wife.
>
> However little known the feelings or views of such a man may be on his first entering a neighborhood, this truth is so well fixed in the minds of the surrounding families that he is considered as the rightful property of some one or other of their daughters. (1)

Some single men, it would appear, have independent access to good fortunes, but all single women or "daughters" must marry for them. "Daughters" and their families, therefore, must think a good deal about marriage while single men with fortunes do not. Families with "daughters" may try to control men too, to seize them as "property," but it is really "daughters," the sentence implies, who are controlled, who are "fixed" by their economic situation. Single men appear at liberty; they can enter a neighborhood and presumably leave it at will. Single men, in short, have an autonomy that "daughters" do not, and at the base of this difference in autonomy is the fact that men have access to money.

That Austen sustains a lively interest in what women and men are worth, that she suggests a causal relation between money and power, sets *Pride and Prejudice* at some distance from *Evelina*, and this distance must be explained in part by historical context. Austen, for example, experienced the effects of industrial capitalism as Burney did not, and one effect of industrial takeoff (which belonged to the late eighteenth and early nineteenth centuries) was to make consciousness of money in general more universal and more respectable as well. One could hardly ignore money, after all, for money was being made and made rapidly in industry and exchange, and money was lending status and power to men who had not had either before, men in trade, for example, men with no pretense at all to the courtly patina of title, family, and long inheritance. This difference in historical context is certainly evoked by the fact that the only tradesmen to appear in *Evelina* are small-time, vulgar, and low, while in *Pride and Prejudice* Mr. and Mrs. Gardiner, living in sight of the Gardiner warehouses, are neither small-time nor vulgar but the most admirable, the most decent, the most well-bred adults in the novel, a fact which the aristocrats must be made to face.

The acquisition of industrial and trading fortunes must also have sharpened money consciousness—and consciousness of the relation between money, status, and power—by increasing the number of men who could actually acquire country estates and merge with the gentry, another change which is expressed in contrasts between *Evelina* and *Pride and Prejudice*. Burney never alludes to the merging of gentry with persons of the middle stations—although this was certainly taking place—and she even mitigates the significance of Evelina's marriage to a lord by revealing, in the nick of time, that Evelina herself is the daughter of a baronet. In *Pride and Prejudice*, however, the merging of gentry and trade is endorsed and even common. Bingley, whose fortune comes from trade and from northern trade at that, is on the verge of finally consolidating his genteel status by purchasing a country estate. Sir William, who has actually retired from trade, has established his family in a country "lodge," and Elizabeth herself, who *is* the daughter of a gentleman but who *does* have connections in business and in the lower regions of the law, marries a man of the upper gentry.

Pride and Prejudice, therefore, evokes the fact that money was being made, that it lent new status and power to men of the middle stations, and that it accelerated the merging of the gentry with the middle classes, and, in its focus on money and money matters, it suggests the concurrence of these phenomena with a sharpened and newly dignified money consciousness. Given this context, it is not surprising that Austen's vision of the power and status of women is persistently linked to their economic situation, as Burney's vision is not. For a general consciousness of the relation between money, status, and power must have had its effect on the way in which the lot of middle-class women was perceived. Of course the lot of middle-class women was also becoming more contradictory, for genteel women continued to lose recognized economic value while genteel men were finding new access to work and new opportunities for rising.[2] The growing contradiction must have been felt as it could not have been felt in the age of Burney.

Austen's personal relation to this larger context certainly increased her consciousness of money in general and of the contradiction between the economic lots of genteel men and women. Although the Austen family was better connected than the Burneys, was distantly related to the aristocracy, and was more immediately related to the clergy, to men in professions (a surgeon and a solicitor), to a lord mayor of London, and to the smaller gentry, Austen felt the pinch of economic stringency when writing *Pride and Prejudice* as Burney did not when writing *Evelina*. Austen's father had died in 1805, and in 1813, the year *Pride and Prejudice* was published, Jane, her mother, and her sister Cassandra were dependent for their living on three sources: a small income of Mrs. Austen's, a small legacy of Cassandra's, and the £250 provided annually by four of the Austen brothers. The sum was enhanced to some degree by the money Jane earned through writing, for in July of that year she reports that "I have now . . . written myself into £250—which only makes me long for more."[3] But the £140 brought by *Sense and Sensibility* and the £110 from *Pride and Prejudice* did not go far, and Austen's letters for that year, as for every year, are full of references to small economies.

In fact, to read Jane Austen's letters—with their steady consciousness of bargains, pence, and shillings—is to be aware of the constancy with which money and money matters impinged upon her own experience as an unmarried woman of the middle stations. In May of 1813, for example, she writes that she is "very lucky" in her gloves, having paid "four shillings," that sarcenet and dimity (at 2/6) are not bargains "but good of their sort," and that a locket at eighteen shillings cost more than Cassandra intended but is "neat and plain, set in gold." In September she is tempted by some edging which is "very cheap" and regretful at having spent six shillings for a white silk handkerchief. She wavers too over some "very pretty English Poplins" (4s/3d), does not buy them, and then decides to treat herself after all with the four pounds which "kind, beautiful" brother Edward has given her. October finds her planning to dye her blue gown, scheming to save Cassandra postage, and inquiring after the price of butcher's meat. In November she notes a fall in the price of bread and hopes that "my Mother's Bill next week will show it."[4]

Austen's family situation, moreover, imposed upon her a heightened awareness of the economic contradiction between the lots of genteel women and genteel men, for Austen had five brothers and they had what she did not: access to work that paid, access to inheritance and privilege, and access to the status that belonged to being prosperous and male. In 1813 all but one brother was rising in a career. James was earning £1,100 a year as a curate, Henry was a partner in a successful banking firm, Frank was the captain of a ship in the Baltic, Charles was the flag captain of another, and Edward, the only brother without a profession, was living as a country gentleman on one of the two estates he had inherited from his adopted family.

The difference which money made in the relative autonomy of Austen women and Austen men was also striking, yet there is little emphatic indication in the letters that unequal economic privilege or unequal power was a source of oppression or discomfort to Jane. Her letters, for the most part, form a casual patchwork of details about her own economies and her brothers' expenditures, about her desire for money and their attainment of it, about her dependence in traveling and their liberties with horseback, carriage, and barouche, about the pressure she felt to marry and the freedom they assumed to marry or not to marry as they chose. Here and there, of course, we find some humorous consciousness of inequity, and there is more than one joke about the economic pressure to marry: "Single Women have a dreadful propensity for being poor—which is one very strong argument in favour of Matrimony."[5] But, for the most part, Jane Austen's attitude toward the economic restrictions of being a woman and toward the resulting absence of autonomy—the dependence, the confinement, the pressure to marry—is, in the letters, amused and uncomplaining.

II

It is in Austen's fiction that we begin to feel an edge, a telling emphasis, being given to the difference between the economic restriction of women and the economic privilege of men. Austen's fiction, like Burney's, was obviously a means of coming to terms with a discomforting experience, was an outlet for critical energies which she could not otherwise express, and those energies are evident in the first sentences of the novel, where Austen implies a relation between money and autonomy which her letters reflect but do not articulate. The outcome of those energies, however, is not what one might expect, for while the rest of the novel does sustain an awareness of the economic inequality of women and men, it does not sustain a felt awareness of the causal connection between money and power. Indeed, for all its reference to money and money matters, for all its consciousness of economic fact and economic influence, *Pride and Prejudice* is devoted not to establishing but to denying the force of economics in human life. In the reading of the novel the real *force* of economics simply melts away.

Despite the first two sentences, despite the implication that access to money in some way determines autonomy, the difference between men's economic privilege and that of women is *not* something we are invited to *experience* as a cause of power and powerlessness in the novel. Men, for all their money and privilege, are not permitted to seem powerful but are rather bungling and absurd; and women, for all their impotence, are not seen as victims of economic restriction. What the novel finally defines as power has little to do with money, and the most authentically powerful figure in the novel is an unmarried middle-class woman without a fortune—a woman, we may note, who bears a striking resemblance to Jane Austen.

While *Evelina* ultimately justifies the control of ruling-class men, *Pride and Prejudice* sustains a fantasy of female autonomy. As in Burney, however, there is no overt indication that Austen protested the economic contradiction on which the inequities of power between men and women were based. Indeed, where the economic inequity of women's lot seems most unfair, Austen is deflecting criticism. Mrs. Bennet and Lady Catherine, for example, are the only persons in the novel allowed to object to the entail, and neither is permitted to engage our sympathies. Mrs. Bennet, in fact, is made to confound potential and plausible criticism by giving it an implausible direction. The entail "was a subject on which Mrs. Bennet was beyond the reach of reason; and she continued to rail bitterly against the cruelty of settling an estate away from a family of five daughters, in favour of a man whom nobody cared anything about" (58). Any reasonable objection to the automatic selection of male inheritors is obscured here by Mrs. Bennet's unreasoning protests.

But if, by deflecting criticism, Austen appears to accept, indeed to apologize for, the unequal division of money and privilege—a division which it would have been futile to protest in 1813—she also appears to limit, subtly and from the outset, what that inequity can mean. Although the Austen of the letters seems well aware of the status and sense of achievement involved in earning or preserving money, she omits from the novel almost any reference to and all observation of activity which has an economic reward. The effect is to mystify one major area in which upper- and middle-class men had access to a sense of power that upper- and middle-class women did not. We do hear that Mr. Bennet oversees the farm, and we know that business prompts Mr. Gardiner to postpone a vacation and to meet with Mr. Stone. We are aware that Darcy writes letters of business and that he cares for his tenants and his library. We understand that

Collins reads, writes sermons, and tends to parish duties, and we are left to imagine that Wickham does something more than gamble in his capacity as officer. But we never see them at work. Both sexes appear only at leisure—eating, reading, attending balls, paying visits, writing personal letters, and playing backgammon, piquet, quadrille, casino, and loo. If the enforced idleness of genteel women seems oppressive in this novel, it is not out of contrast with the more productive activities of males.

It is principally in their personal rather than in their working lives that men appear at first to have more autonomy than women, more power to make decisions, to go and to do as they please. Throughout *Pride and Prejudice* men have a mobility that women, even women with money, do not, and that mobility suggests a greater general self-rule. From the first sentence on, men are linked with entry and removal, women with being "fixed." Bingley, for example, first enters the scene in a chaise and four and then leaves almost immediately for London, prompting Mrs. Bennet to worry—in woman's traditional fashion—that he will "be always flying about from one place to another" (7). Bingley, in fact, prides himself on his alacrity in leaving—". . . if I should resolve to quit Netherfield, I should probably be off in five minutes"—and he does leave Jane abruptly and painfully, only to saunter up again some ten months later (39). Bingley's mobility is typical of that of the other single men in the novel, for the militia too enter and then leave, as do Wickham, Collins, and Darcy.

Women, in contrast, do not usually enter or leave at all except in the wake of men. The Miss Bingleys move with their brother; Lydia pursues the regiment; and Charlotte Lucas, Lydia, Elizabeth, and Jane all follow the men they marry. Lady Catherine's rude excursion to Meryton, Jane's visit to London, and Elizabeth's to Hunsford and Derbyshire are seen as deviations from the more usual pattern of women's self-initiated activity, the movements back and forth within a small radius, "the walks to Meryton, sometimes dirty and sometimes cold" (143). So limited is women's usual movement—the walk to Meryton is only a mile—that a walk of three miles, at a rapid pace and without a companion, is an event. Indeed, women's usual state is not to move at all but to hear news or to read letters about the arrivals and departures of males. At most, perhaps, women look out of a window or throw up a sash, but they are essentially "fixed," and it is not surprising that it is women in the novel who are dull or bored, who feel that the country is "bare of news," who suffer when it rains, who repine at "the dullness of everything," who feel "forlorn" (25, 223, 311).

The patterns of movement in the novel do suggest a dramatic difference between the autonomy of women and men as the patterns of movement in *Evelina* do not. But they are finally background, like the fact that men work, and they are neither emphasized nor overthrown. It is in relation to the marriage choice that men's potential autonomy is brought most into conscious focus, and it is in relation to the marriage choice that their autonomy is also most emphatically subverted. As the first two sentences of the novel suggest, men do not need to marry. They may "want" or desire wives, as it turns out, but they do not *need* to want them as women must want husbands. Men in *Pride and Prejudice*, therefore, are conscious of having the power to choose and they are fond of dwelling on it, of impressing it upon women. Mr. Collins, for example, assumes that there is nothing so central to his proposal as a rehearsal of his "reasons" for marrying—and for choosing a Bennet in particular—nothing quite so central as the information that there were "many amiable young women" from whom he might have made his selection (101, 102).

Darcy is scarcely less agreeably aware of his power to choose, and from his first appearance he acts the role of high-class connoisseur, finding Elizabeth "tolerable; but not handsome enough to tempt *me*" (9). Like Mr. Collins, moreover,

Darcy remains preoccupied with the privilege of choice in the very act of proposing, for his first words are not "I love you" but "in vain have I struggled" (178). Bingley, Colonel Fitzwilliam, and Wickham, the other single men in the novel, betray a similar consciousness. Bingley chooses his male friend over Jane. Fitzwilliam maintains that "younger sons cannot marry where they like," but Elizabeth protests that they often choose to like and to propose to "women of fortune" (173). And Wickham, ever confident in his power to choose, first chooses Georgiana Darcy and then, in succession, Elizabeth Bennet, Mary King, and Lydia Bennet.

Male privilege, then, and access to money in particular, makes men feel autonomous. It also makes them feel empowered to control others, especially the women to whom they make advances. For, as givers of economic benefits, men expect their advances to be received and even sought after. Mr. Collins dwells warmly upon the "advantages that are in [his] power to offer" and tactfully reminds Elizabeth that she is bound to accept him, for ". . . it is by no means certain that another offer of marriage may ever be made you. Your portion is unhappily so small that it will in all likelihood undo the effects of your loveliness and amiable qualifications" (102, 104).

Darcy is also pleasantly aware of his power to bestow value, whether it is his desirable attention or his desirable fortune and station. At the first ball, for example, he will not dance with Elizabeth because he says he is in "no humour at present to give consequence to young ladies who are slighted by other men" (9). His first proposal—like Mr. Collins'—is "not more eloquent on the subject of tenderness than of pride," and it betrays his confidence in having his way: "[Elizabeth] could easily see that he had no doubt of a favourable answer. He *spoke* of apprehension and anxiety, but his countenance expressed real security" (179).

Mr. Bennet, too, seems to relish the power he has over women and to seek opportunities for its display. Aware of having wasted his power of choice by choosing Mrs. Bennet, he is fond of reminding his wife and his daughters that he has control over their economic well-being: "[The letter] is from my cousin, Mr. Collins, who, when I am dead, may turn you all out of this house as soon as he pleases" (58). Indeed, with the possible exceptions of Bingley, who is seen as an anomaly, and of Mr. Gardiner, who scarcely exists, virtually every man in the novel reacts in the same fashion to his economic privilege and social status as a male. All enjoy a mobility which women do not have. All relish an autonomy which women do not feel. All aspire to a mastery which women cannot grasp. And yet, in spite of their mobility, their sense of autonomy, and their desire to master and control, we do not feel that men are powerful in this novel. Their sense of power and their real pomposity are at base a setup, a preparation for poetic justice, a license to enjoy the spectacle of men witlessly betraying their legacy of power, of men demonstrating impressive capacities for turning potential control into ineffective action and submission to the control of others.

It is significant, I think, that the only proposals of marriage recorded in the novel are unsuccessful and that both suitors are so immersed in their sense of control that they blindly offend the woman whose affections they mean to attach and, in the process, provoke what must be two of the most vigorous rejections in all literature. Here is Elizabeth to Mr. Collins: "You could not make *me* happy, and I am convinced that I am the last woman in the world who would make *you* so" (103). And here is Elizabeth to Mr. Darcy: "I had not known you a month before I felt that you were the last man in the world whom I could ever be prevailed on to marry" (182).[6] It is also significant that two of the men in the novel who have risen through preference—another benefit of male privilege—enjoy little more than an inflated *sense* of control and succeed mainly in annoying those whom they propose to act upon. Sir William, who has "risen to the honour of knighthood" and retired to Meryton, "where he could think with pleasure of his own importance," does no more than provoke Darcy when he attempts to claim his society (15); Mr. Collins may enjoy "the consequential feelings of early and unexpected prosperity," and he may persuade Charlotte Lucas to marry him, but he is thwarted in his attempts to act upon Elizabeth, Darcy, Mr. Bennet, and even Lydia and Kitty (66).

Our sense of male control is also undercut by the comic readiness with which some men submit to the control of others. Mr. Collins and Sir William both manifest such slavish admiration of those who have raised them or of those who stand above them in rank that their own imagined power is constantly and ironically juxtaposed with images of self-abasement: picture Sir William "stationed in the doorway, in earnest contemplation of the greatness before him," or Collins carving, eating, and praising "as if he felt that life could furnish nothing greater" (151, 154). Collins, moreover, qualifies his potential autonomy by submitting virtually every decision to the "particular advice and recommendation" of Lady Catherine, and Bingley surrenders Jane because he depends on Darcy's opinion more strongly than on his own (101). Men are also prone to misusing their autonomy by making bad investments. Mr. Bennet's own imprudence must account for his unhappy domestic life, and Wickham's failure of resolution yokes him to Lydia, a giddy woman without a fortune. Thus access to money and male privilege in general do grant men the potential for control of their lives and for control over women, but, against the background of their real physical mobility, the men in *Pride and Prejudice* are essentially set up—to surrender, to misuse, to fail to realize the power that is their cultural legacy.[7]

In obvious contrast to men, women, in their economic dependence, have far less potential to do as they like. Most women in the novel *must* marry, and, since access to money both shapes and is shaped by traditional attitudes toward women and their proper destiny, even women with money feel pressured to get a man (the rich Miss Bingley pursues Darcy, as does Lady Catherine on behalf of the wealthy Anne). Women, for the most part, do not dwell on their power to choose, do not debate over getting a husband, and seldom give thought to the value of one husband over another. Some young women, like Lydia and Kitty, are so engrossed with male regard in general that they lose sight of their reason for securing it, which is to marry, and make the attention of men—any men—an end in itself.

Indeed, the action in almost the entire first volume of the novel consists of very little but women talking or thinking or scheming about men. There is the initial plot to meet Bingley, then the first ball with its triumphs and failures. This is followed by a review of who was admired most, by a conversation between Elizabeth and Charlotte about how Jane had best pursue Bingley, by another scheme to keep Jane in Bingley's range at Netherfield, and by Miss Bingley's pursuit of Darcy at Netherfield itself. In the meantime we also hear that the militia have arrived and that Kitty and Lydia are well supplied with "news and happiness" (25). Wickham appears; Wickham is schemed over; and the whole first movement of the novel is brought to a close with another ball and another flourish of female display.[8]

The degree of female obsession with men, the degree to which they lack autonomy or self-control, may also be measured by the degree to which they helplessly and unthinkingly discount their ties to one another when a man's attention is at stake. Caroline Bingley, of course, is the most extreme example. Her abuse of Elizabeth is unrelenting, and her friendliness and her sister's friendliness to Jane wax and wane with the absence or restoration of male regard: ". . . when the gentlemen entered, Jane was no longer the first object" (50). Even sisterly affection is tenuous where men are concerned. Kitty and Lydia set off to inquire about Captain Carter but not to visit the ailing Jane. Kitty can only weep "from vexation and envy" when Lydia goes to Brighton, and Lydia herself is fond of twitting her sisters about having married before them (298). So languid is one sister's interest in another that, when Bingley and Darcy dine away from Netherfield, Caroline summons Jane on the grounds that "a whole day's tête-à-tête between two women can never end without a quarrel" (27).

Women in *Pride and Prejudice*, then, do not generally act like choosers, and, since they devote a good deal of energy to compulsive scheming and plotting, they obviously do not entertain illusions of easy control. What power women do aspire to is manipulative and indirect and is further diminished by the fact that obsession makes them ineffective and unreflecting. Mrs. Bennet, for example, frustrates her own ends time and time again while entertaining "the delightful persuasion" that she is promoting Jane's marriage (99). Miss Bingley's pathetic snares entangle not Darcy but herself. Mary's eagerness for display blinds her to the embarrassment of her "pedantic air," and Lydia's passion for the attentions of a charming male wins her a husband who must be bribed to marry her and whose affection for her "soon sunk into indifference" (22, 366).

It is important to note, however, that we are not just speaking of the Mrs. Bennets, the Carolines, the Lydias, and the Marys, for all young women in the novel are caught to some degree in the same currents, and this enforces our sense of a universal female condition. All the Bennet women spend a good part of one evening conjecturing about Bingley and "determining when they should ask him to dinner" (6). All are pleased with their own or with each other's triumphs. All are bored by the "interval of waiting" for the gentlemen, and the prospect of the Netherfield ball is "extremely agreeable to every female of the family" (72, 92). Our first introduction to Elizabeth, in fact, finds her trimming a hat.

Women, like men, therefore appear to be determined almost uniformly by a shared economic and social condition, but, just as we are not permitted to feel that men's economic privilege necessitates power, so are we not permitted to feel that women's lack of privilege necessitates powerlessness. The first two sentences of the novel may emphasize the idea that women's compulsive husband hunting has an economic base, but we are never allowed to *feel* that base as a determining force in their experience. As I have suggested, almost every reference in the novel to economic necessity is relegated to Mrs. Bennet, a woman whose worries we are not allowed to take seriously because they are continually undermined by their link with the comic and the absurd: ". . . Miss Lizzy, if you take it into your head to go on refusing every offer of marriage in this way, you will never get a husband at all—and I am sure I do not know who is to maintain you when your father is dead" (108–109). This is the kind of financial threat which would be taken seriously in a novel by Charlotte Brontë, but in *Pride and Prejudice* this threat, this sting of potential poverty, is undercut. There is consciousness of economics, to be sure, but that consciousness is raised and then subverted.[9] This is an odd maneuver on the part of an author sometimes praised for her awareness of social and economic forces, but it serves a purpose as preparation for Elizabeth by defining the nature of Elizabeth's world.

The Charlotte Lucas episode is especially significant in this light, for at a distance it might suggest that economic forces do indeed have tragic domination over "sensible, intelligent" young women (15). But once again this is not what we are actually invited to feel. We are not allowed to dwell on the economic realities of Charlotte's situation, because the shifting ironies almost continually direct us elsewhere: we look with irony at Mr. Collins, for example, or at Charlotte's family, or at Charlotte herself. When her economic considerations *are* introduced, they are introduced ironically and at her expense: "Miss Lucas . . . accepted him solely from the pure and disinterested desire of an establishment" (117).

If we feel sympathy for Charlotte at any point, we first do so when her family dwells on the economic and social advantages of the match and gives no thought at all to her personal happiness. To Sir William and Lady Lucas the fulsome Mr. Collins is "a most eligible match for their daughter, to whom they could give little fortune" (117). Charlotte's brothers are relieved of their fear that she will become a financial burden, "an old maid," and her younger sisters "formed hopes of *coming out* a year or two sooner," in order we presume to strike their own marital bargains (118). But these ironies still do not put us in contact with her economic necessities. They may expose the selfishness and money-mindedness of Charlotte's relations, but if anything the suggestion that Charlotte's family is overly concerned with money puts us at a greater distance from any real sense of Charlotte's economic needs.

It is in the paragraph on Charlotte's own reflections that we come closest to seeing her as the victim of those economic and social forces which tend to reduce genteel unmarried women to the status of merchandise:

> Without thinking highly either of men or of matrimony, marriage had always been her object; it was the only honourable provision for well-educated young women of small fortune, and however uncertain of giving happiness, must be their pleasantest preservation from want. This preservative she had now obtained; and at the age of twenty-seven, without having ever been handsome, she felt all the good luck of it. (118)

The reference here to marriage as the "only honourable provision" evokes a strong pull of sympathy for Charlotte but, coming as it does in the midst of her other reflections, it is not entirely clear to what extent the narrator joins her in this point of view. The extent to which we *can* feel the authority of this reference is the extent to which we will feel the force of economic necessity in Charlotte's decision, but the authority of the reference is never clear.

Elizabeth's own judgment lays the blame for Charlotte's decision on Charlotte's perversity: "She had always felt that Charlotte's opinion of matrimony was not exactly like her own, but she could not have supposed it possible that when called into action she would have sacrificed every better feeling to worldly advantage" (121). Yet the extent to which Elizabeth's judgment has narrative authority is also cloudy. Certainly, Elizabeth can be accused of speaking from fear, fear that Charlotte's example is a portent of her own fate as a single woman of small fortune. And certainly Elizabeth is inconsistent, for she defends Wickham for the same behavior with Mary King. If we see Charlotte with irony, we see Elizabeth with irony too, and ultimately the narrator abandons us to ambivalence. The Charlotte Lucas episode, on the whole, is left to suggest, on the one hand, the perverting force of women's economic lot and to prevent us, on the other, from feeling that force as a reality in the universe of Elizabeth Bennet.[10]

One effect of undermining the force of economic realities is to make most women, in their helpless fixation on men and marriage, look perverse or merely silly and to lay the blame on women themselves, not on their economic and social lot. Another effect, however, is to suggest, rather wishfully, that there is some way out. Men may go about acting more powerful than women—indeed, their lot in life may give them the potential for having power—but because a sense of power seems to befuddle critical vision they are not really powerful at all. Conversely, women may seem powerless as men are not, but because we are finally not to *feel* that they are victims of social and economic forces they do not have to be powerless after all. What we have in *Pride and Prejudice*, it seems, is a novel that recognizes the shaping influence of economics but that denies its force. The novel, in fact, all but levels what in life we know to have been the material base of power and powerlessness and defines real power as something separate from the economic.

III

Real power in *Pride and Prejudice*, as is often observed, involves having the intelligence, the wit, and the critical attitudes of Jane Austen; and Elizabeth Bennet, as it is also sometimes observed, is essentially an Austen fantasy, a fantasy of power.[11] As a fantasy, of course, Austen's Elizabeth is to some extent like Burney's Evelina: the nature of her power is traditional and womanly; it is the power of autonomy and, specifically, the power of private opinion and self-defense. Elizabeth's opinions, however, are not so private as Evelina's. They are not confined to letters, nor, as a matter of fact, are they confined to novels. For Elizabeth's world, as created by Jane Austen, affords her a freedom which Austen's world evidently did not. It affords her scope not only to entertain critical attitudes but to express them with energy and to put them into effective action. Elizabeth can do more than quietly scorn Miss Bingley's eagerness to please Darcy—she can laugh out loud at Jane's gratitude for being admired, and she can reject outright Charlotte's schemes for securing a husband. She can put herself at some distance from gratefulness, scheming, and overeagerness to please men, and in the process she can also be rather direct and effective in challenging Darcy's traditional assumption of control as a ruling-class man.

Elizabeth's world, in contrast to Austen's, permits her something more than spiritual victories, permits her more than that *sense* of autonomy which comes with wittily observing the confinements of one's situation, with standing apart from them in spirit while having to bend to them in daily behavior. It permits her not only the energetic expression of but also the forceful use of those critical energies which Austen herself diverted into novels and which Evelina confines, more or less, to correspondence. Austen's fantasy of female autonomy is far more rebellious, then, than Fanny Burney's, for Elizabeth's autonomy, although a version of those "private opinions" which even "yoked creatures" entertain, is still a version which allows them rather free expression and, most important, which allows them to modify the power relations in Elizabeth's world.

If in *Evelina* the most central expression of power is that of landed male control, in *Pride and Prejudice* the most prominent form of power is that of female autonomy, and it is not implausible to see in this distance between Burney and Austen an expression of the changing social context. Austen, for example, in allowing female autonomy to work effectively against a ruling-class male—a use of power entirely foreign to *Evelina*—evokes a more general sense that the authority of landed males had been challenged if not actually mitigated. In her endorsement of an autonomy not tied to class or fortune, Austen also reveals some affinity with an individualism that had ties to the French and the Industrial revolutions. This individualism is usually identified as middle-class and, by implication too, as male, and it is usually discussed in its economic application. Eric Hobsbawm, for example, sees "individualist competition, the 'career open to talent,' and the triumph of merit over birth and connexion" as a significant result of the dual revolutions, but the "career open to talent" is a concept which applies only to men and for the most part to men of the middle class.[12] John Owen also refers to the early nineteenth century as a "new era of individualism and *laissez-faire*," another definition of "individualism" which emphasizes the growing economic privileges of middle-class men.[13] And Ian Watt, in his discussion of "individualism and the novel," focuses upon "economic individualism" as represented in the "economic man"—although in this case "economic man" includes Moll Flanders, a low-life female.[14]

The individualism or autonomy of Austen's heroine, however, is adapted to the purposes of a genteel unmarried woman. It is not expressed, therefore, through economic achievement, as it might be in a male, nor is it expressed through grand actions upon the world. It is an individualism, moreover, that cannot really be defined as middle-class or antigentry, for it is tied less to Austen's class sympathies than to her partially articulated feelings as a woman—the energy of Elizabeth's critical opinions, for example, is directed against men of middle stations, like Collins and Wickham, not just against the upper-class Darcy. Elizabeth's individualism, that is, is often directed against those very men of the middle stations, those men rising in careers, who conventionally define for us what individualism means. Austen's adaptation of individualism is thus more feminist than middle-class, for it is a disguised expression of discontent with the growing division in money, status, and power between middle-class men and middle-class women.

Elizabeth's autonomy, then, expresses an individualism adapted to female use, but because it is so adapted it is also heavily qualified and disguised, much as Evelina's far less developed powers are qualified and disguised by Fanny Burney. And the most potent qualification of Elizabeth's autonomy lies in the nature of the fictional world that Austen has created on her behalf. That we enjoy Elizabeth's critical energies as we do, that we feel safe with them, and that generations of conventional readers have found her charming rather than reckless owe much to the fact that Austen's version of Elizabeth's universe is one which mitigates the punishing potential of her critical views and challenging behavior. If money, for example, were really a force in the novel, we might find Elizabeth heedless, radical, or at best naïve for insulting and rejecting a man with £10,000 a year, for condemning her best friend, a plain and portionless twenty-seven-year-old, because she married a man who could support her in comfort. In similar fashion, if wealthy young men were less given to bungling and dissipating the autonomy and control that are their legacy, we might feel uncomfortable or incredulous when Elizabeth takes on Darcy. It is Austen's subversion of economic realities and of male power that permits us to enjoy Elizabeth's rebellious exuberance, because it is principally this subversion which limits, from the outset, the extent to which we feel Elizabeth is in conflict with the forces of her world.

But to allow a nineteenth-century heroine to get away with being critical and challenging—especially about male control and feminine submission—is still to rebel against ideology and dominant social relations, no matter how charmingly that heroine may be represented, no matter how safe her rebellion is made to appear. When Austen allows Elizabeth to express critical attitudes and to act upon them without penalty, she is moving against early nineteenth-century ideologies about feminine behavior and feminine fate, for by any traditional standards Elizabeth's departures from convention ought to earn her a life of spinsterhood, not a man, a carriage, and £10,000 a year. Elizabeth's universe, moreover, is real enough—its economic and social forces are kept close enough to the surface—that we believe in it and do not dismiss it as fantasy. And Elizabeth herself is so convincing that we can't dismiss her either. For all its charm and relative safety, Elizabeth's rebellion invites us to take it seriously, and it is for this reason, I assume, that the rebelliousness of *Pride and Prejudice*, like the rebelliousness of most women's writing, is even further qualified.

One major qualification of Elizabeth's resistance to male control, to men's assumption of control, and to women's submissive behavior is that, like Austen, she accepts the basic division in men's and women's economic lots. Men have a right to money that women do not. Thus Wickham is prudent for pursuing Mary King, but Charlotte is mercenary for marrying Collins. Men also have a right to greater autonomy, to greater power of choice, for Elizabeth never does challenge Darcy's ideologically justified right to criticize women or to act the connoisseur. Nor is it entirely clear that she objects to men's general assumption of control over women. Her real aim is self-defense; she wants to resist intimidation and to deny Darcy's particular assumption of control over her, a control which he exercises through the expression of critical judgments: "He has a very satirical eye, and if I do not begin by being impertinent myself, I shall soon grow afraid of him" (21).

Elizabeth's habitual tactic with Darcy is to anticipate and to deflate him in the role of critic and chooser but never to challenge the privilege by which he is either one. One of her maneuvers is to insinuate her own judgment before Darcy can deliver his: "Did not you think, Mr. Darcy, that I expressed myself uncommonly well just now . . ." (21). Another is to deprive him of the opportunity to judge at all: ". . . he means to be severe on us, and our surest way of disappointing him, will be to ask nothing about it" (52). And still another is to defy him outright: ". . . despise me if you dare" (48). Elizabeth's witty portraits of Darcy are also designed to cast doubt upon his reliability as critic but not upon his right to criticize. Darcy's pride and his alleged indifference to friendship, for example, must make him overly harsh and therefore untrustworthy in his judgments: "And *your* defect is a propensity to hate every body" (54).

Elizabeth, of course, in defending herself against the controlling power of Darcy's negative judgments, suggests that she is also defending herself against a desire to please Darcy and to enjoy the benefit of his positive attentions. Her defense, that is, continually implies an underlying vulnerability to his good opinion, and this is another qualification of her autonomy. Elizabeth never challenges the privilege by which Darcy bestows benefit through his regard, never entirely denies the benefit he does bestow, and is never wholly immune to enjoying it. She merely tries to avoid responding to his attentions with that show of gratefulness and pleasure which he egoistically expects and which her own feelings indeed prompt in her. At Netherfield, when Darcy asks her to dance, she is at first "amazed at the dignity to which she [had] arrived," but her overriding defensive purpose is to deny both to herself and to him that the occasion affords her any sense of status or pleasure (86). It is evident, then, that Elizabeth's resistance to Darcy is undermined by a lingering susceptibility to his attentions and by a lingering desire to please. In fact, the very energy with which she defends herself against both pleasing and being pleased argues that she is not only vulnerable to Darcy's power over her feelings but ironically and defensively controlled by it.

Elizabeth's qualified opposition to being controlled by one attractive male is juxtaposed, moreover, with her complete vulnerability to the emotional control of another, for she succumbs to pleasing Wickham and being flattered by him even before he reveals himself as an ally. Indeed, Elizabeth's readiness to believe Wickham is partially explained by the fact that, like all the young women in the novel, she is ready to approve any attractive and charming man who pays her attention, to decide absurdly that his "very countenance may vouch for [his] being amiable" (77). Elizabeth's head is full not only of what Wickham tells her about Darcy but of Wickham himself, and in dressing for the Netherfield ball she thinks both of "seeing a confirmation of every thing in Mr. Darcy's looks and behaviour" and of conquering "all that remained unsubdued of [Wickham's] heart" (80, 85). Even after Wickham has thrown her over for Mary King, or Mary King's fortune, she continues to be flattered by "a solicitude, an interest which she felt must ever attach her to him with a most sincere regard" (144).

As it turns out, of course, Elizabeth is not only not autonomous with Darcy and Wickham, she is mistaken and wrong.

She is wrong about Darcy's intentions, and she is wrong about Wickham's, and she is wrong for the same reason that she is not self-directing. Despite her intelligence, wit, and critical energies, she cares too much about male regard.[15] As she herself is aware, after reading Darcy's letter, it is her "vanity," her vulnerability to the good opinion of men, that has blinded her both to Darcy's character and to Wickham's:

> But vanity, not love, has been my folly. Pleased with the preference of one and offended by the neglect of the other, on the very beginning of our acquaintance, I have courted prepossession and ignorance and driven reason away where either were concerned. (196)

If there is any punch left in Elizabeth's resistance to Darcy's traditional assumptions of control, it is certainly diminished by our continuing awareness that the rebellion itself works in the interests of tradition. That is, Elizabeth's assertion of autonomy attracts Darcy rather than putting him off. Elizabeth, we are assured, has a "mixture of sweetness and archness in her manner which made it difficult for her to affront anybody; and Darcy had never been so bewitched by any woman as he was by her" (48). Heightened aggression on Elizabeth's part is met by heightened feeling on Darcy's, by greater fears of "the danger of paying Elizabeth too much attention" (54). Thus we may enjoy Elizabeth's self-assertions, but we are never invited to value them in themselves, as we are invited by later novelists to value Jane Eyre's or Lucy Snowe's or Maggie Tulliver's. Elizabeth's qualified resistance to Darcy, attractive as relief from the extreme male centering of most women in the novel, is valued in great measure, nevertheless, because it attracts the attention of a desirable man.

Elizabeth's autonomy, then, is quiet, is not intended to alarm. It invites the conventional female reader to identify with unconventional energies but commits her to nothing more, and it permits the conventional male reader to admire Elizabeth's spirit while finding comfort in the fact that she is wrong, that she is not autonomous after all, and that her whole resistance to male control only secures and gives value to the love of a good man. It is as if Austen could not be indirect or qualified enough in presenting this self-assertive heroine, for we almost never focus on Elizabeth's rebellious energies without feeling the undermining force of one irony or another. It is, in fact, Austen's qualification of Elizabeth's power that accounts for most of the complexities and ironies in the first two-thirds of the novel, and it is these ironies, I suspect, that have permitted the most conventional readers to find Elizabeth charming—and most charming of all when she asserts her independence of Darcy's traditional control as a male.

As a power fantasy, Elizabeth is in some ways astoundingly modest. The remarkable thing, perhaps, is that her rebelliousness, undercut and qualified as it is, still maintains a quality of force, still strikes us as power. It does so in part because of its juxtaposition with Miss Bingley's ineffective machinations and Jane's well-intentioned passivity, both reminders of what it means to be traditionally feminine. And in part, too, Elizabeth's rebellious energies retain a quality of force because they really act upon her world; they change Darcy, change the way he responds to his economic and social privileges, change something basic to the power relation between him and Elizabeth. Without intending to, Elizabeth exercises influence over Darcy, renders him more courtly, less liable to impress upon her the power he has to choose and to give her benefits, and less liable to assume control of her feelings. Evelina, in contrast, must depend upon the purely voluntary goodness of Lord Orville.

Still, neither Elizabeth's much qualified self-defense nor even her unintended influence over Darcy establishes her as the powerful character she is. The most profound source of what we feel as Elizabeth's power is her ability—in the last third of the novel—to turn her critical vision upon herself, upon her own unthinking vulnerability to male approval. It is at this point in the novel that Elizabeth establishes what we could call real autonomy. It is at this point, moreover—the point at which Elizabeth redirects her critical energies from Darcy to herself—that the multiple ironies which have characterized the first two-thirds of the novel are suddenly dropped. It is a less anxiety-provoking business for a woman to assert autonomy against an aspect of herself, against the enemy within, than against the traditional power relations of her culture. And though it is necessary and vital to assess one's own blindness, in a patriarchal society, this is also a much surer and more lasting form of power than pitting one's self against the traditional privileges of men.

Elizabeth's recognition of her vulnerability to male attention does force her, however, into painful and even humiliating recognitions. It is a hard thing for a woman who has felt herself defended against the control of a ruling-class man to discover, after all, that she has been led astray by her extreme vulnerability to his good opinion. It is humiliating to feel apologetic toward an oppressor—for Darcy has greater control than Elizabeth and has made her feel it. Why has Austen put her through this? One answer, perhaps, is that Elizabeth's recognition of her "vanity" further undercuts her rebellion against male control. But her confessions may also be seen as a hard lesson in the difficulties of confronting the enemy within, a hard lesson in the fact that the most apparently autonomous women may be creatures of their culture too.

This lesson is especially painful and realistic because, despite Austen's ironic underminings, the force of Elizabeth's community is strongly felt. But in this novel, in contrast say to Brontë's *Villette*, the shaping force of community is evoked only to be dramatically overthrown. The degree to which Elizabeth has been immersed in the values and mystifications of her community is the degree to which we feel that she is powerful when she separates herself from both.

IV

Pride and Prejudice brings to a culmination the kind of quest plot which is only initiated and then dropped in *Evelina*, for by the end of this novel the heroine has achieved real autonomy and self-direction; indeed, no other character in the novel achieves her measure of self-knowledge or potential self-rule. The self-knowledge which comes to Darcy comes to him offstage and at the instigation of Elizabeth. Elizabeth alone is her own analyst and, in a novel where Austen brilliantly arranges for intelligence to mitigate the forces of economics and social position, Elizabeth emerges for the readers as the most powerful because the most intelligent and self-directing character in the novel. But if, in reading Darcy's letter, Elizabeth gains a measure of real autonomy, in that she gains a measure of freedom from the unthinking desire for male regard, what Elizabeth's freedom finally purchases is an ability to consider, to weigh, to choose which male's regard she really values. Elizabeth's autonomy, that is, frees her to choose Darcy, and her untraditional power is rewarded not with some different life but with woman's traditional life, with love and marriage. Quest in this novel is partly justified by and then rewarded with love.

The economic contradiction of men's and women's lives, the paucity of options for genteel women at the time, the weight of ideology as expressed in life and fiction permit Austen no other happy ending, but there is of course a major difficulty in Elizabeth's reward. For marriage in this novel, as in life, involves a power relation between unequals, and that is hardly a fitting end for a fantasy of power. What we find at the end of *Pride and Prejudice*, therefore, is a complicated and not entirely successful juggling act in which all the economic privilege and social authority of the traditional husband-hero must be demonstrated at last but demonstrated without diminishing the autonomy of the heroine.

It is not until late in the novel, for example, not until Elizabeth rejects Darcy's proposal, reads his letter, and establishes herself as the most powerful character in the book, that we are permitted firsthand exposure to Darcy's economic and social significance. Only at Pemberley, for example, are we made to *feel* the reality of his authority to act upon the world: "As a brother, a landlord, a master, she considered . . . How much of pleasure or pain it was in his power to bestow" (234). Darcy's authority, moreover, is juxtaposed on this visit with the first signs that he has been influenced by Elizabeth's self-assertion: "Never in her life had she seen his manners so little dignified, never had he spoken with such gentleness as on this unexpected meeting" (235).

Darcy's rescue of Lydia is another demonstration of the hero's traditional authority, the authority belonging to money, class, and male privilege, but it is also to be construed as further demonstration that Elizabeth has influenced him, that he is more courtly not only to her but to her family, whom he is now not above serving. Darcy's second proposal, moreover, is brought on by still another spirited assertion of Elizabeth's autonomy, her refusal to conciliate Lady Catherine, and even the timing of this proposal scene is set by Elizabeth. The proposal itself, finally, is followed by Darcy's lengthy reminder that it is Elizabeth who has changed him: "You taught me a lesson, hard indeed at first but most advantageous. By you I was properly humbled" (349).

But it "will never do" for Elizabeth to seem more powerful than Darcy (361). That is not what traditional marriages, what "good" marriages, are all about. According to Mr. Bennet, in fact, Elizabeth "could be neither happy nor respectable unless [she] truly esteemed [her] husband, unless [she] looked up to him as a superior" (356). Darcy must protest, then, that he would have proposed whether Elizabeth opened the way or not: "I was not in a humor to wait for any opening of yours" (361). And Elizabeth, for her part, must betray some consciousness of and gratefulness for the traditional economic and social benefits. She must appreciate Pemberley not just for the good taste that it exhibits but for its economic grandeur,[16] for the "very large" park and for the "lofty and handsome" rooms (228, 229). She must acknowledge that to be mistress of Pemberley might be "something," and she must experience "gratitude" to Darcy for loving her (228, 248). Yet Elizabeth's own autonomy must not be diminished. She is allowed, therefore, to see more than Darcy does to the last:[17] "She remembered that he had yet to learn to be laughed at, and it was rather too early to begin" (351). We leave her, in fact, in the last paragraph of the novel, surrounded by Pemberley's splendor but seeming to hold her own, astonishing Georgiana with her "lively, sportive manner" and her "open pleasantry" and persuading Darcy, against his will, to make peace with Lady Catherine (367).

Austen's difficulties with Elizabeth's reward, her attempt to give her marriage but to alter what marriage means, her attempt to balance love and quest, her tinkering with heroine and hero must account for the fact that most readers of *Pride and Prejudice* find the end less satisfactory than the beginning. On the one hand, the charge that Elizabeth, as witty heroine, is now too inclined to moralize and be grateful owes much to the fact that marriage requires her to dwindle by degrees into a wife. On the other hand, the observation that Darcy as hero is less convincing than as villain owes much to the requirements of Austen's fantasy, which are that Elizabeth not dwindle too far, that she maintain her equality with if not her ascendancy over her husband.[18] Darcy, therefore, though he must demonstrate all the economic privilege and social authority of the traditional hero—which are plenty—may not have everything; he may not have Pemberley, £10,000 a year, rank, looks, intelligence, flexibility, wit, and a convincing reality as well. There is some point, though an unconscious point, to his stiffness and unreality, for both function at some level to preserve the fantasy of Elizabeth's power.

The end of *Pride and Prejudice,* nevertheless, witnesses a decline in Elizabeth Bennet, for in *Pride and Prejudice* as in much of women's fiction the end, the reward, of woman's apprenticeship to life is marriage, and marriage demands resignation even as it prompts rejoicing, initiates new life while it confirms a flickering suspicion that the best is over. Given the ambivalent blessing of marriage as a happy ending, it is a tribute to Austen's genius that what we take from *Pride and Prejudice* is not a sense of Elizabeth's untimely decline but a tonic impression of her intelligence, her wit, and her power, and it is an even greater tribute that we believe in her power, that we do not perceive it as fantasy. For Austen's brilliant construction of her heroine's world, her recognition and subtle subversion of economic forces, the mobile intelligence of the heroine herself, the ironies directed at that intelligence, the complexities of Elizabeth's failure in vision and of her recovery complicate what is at base a wish fulfillment, give it an air of credibility which lends force to the spell of the fantasy upon us.

As one of my students put it, we need more fantasies like Elizabeth.

3. *Villette*

Villette begins in that ideal interior, those "large" and "well-proportioned"[1] rooms, which in *Pride and Prejudice* and in much fiction by women functions as an emblem of the heroine's reward at the end of the novel—the life of comfort, quiet, and order conventionally supposed to define the experience of a genteel married woman. Like many heroines before her, Lucy Snowe appears well pleased at first with the emotional tenor of this life, a tenor suggested by the calm interior of the Bretton house, by "the large, peaceful rooms, the well-arranged furniture, the clear, wide windows," and by the housewife herself, a figure most pointedly represented by Polly Home.[2] Polly, of course, is only a child of seven, but she is a child who is learning how to be a woman, and in great measure she already behaves like an upper-middle-class housewife—stirring cream and sugar into papa's tea and meeting Graham at the end of a hard day with a warning to wipe his shoes properly upon the mat. Scolding, comforting, attending, Polly is intensely familiar, a doll-sized version of the genteel married woman and a figure in whom all the daily business and daily relations of a dependent female appear officially charming.

Many readers of *Villette* have responded to this charm and have been inclined to see in the first three chapters one of the least unpleasant episodes in the troubled history of Lucy Snowe—Andrew Hook, for example, finds the Bretton house "an asylum of peace and tranquillity."[3] But, for all its surface attractions, the Bretton household is not as tranquil as it has been seen: the very quiet of its interior is the quiet of muted suffering, and at the base of Polly's ostensibly charming relation to Graham is a power dynamic which is distinctly unpleasant. Charlotte Brontë, in fact, without making any overt comment to the effect, quietly presents the dependent life, the traditional end point of a marriage plot, as a condensation of powerlessness and pain.

Although there is much in Brontë's portrait of the dependent life that is familiar from Jane Austen, the inequities of money and power which Brontë subtly evokes are more permanent, more radical, and more painful than the inequities of money and power which Austen establishes and then subverts in *Pride and Prejudice*. In Brontë, for example, the economic inequity between men and women, which is based not on men's access to money but on their access to work that pays, is never mystified or subverted. Men's work and most women's lack of work are real to us in this novel, and, because they are real, we are made to experience what we are never really permitted to feel in *Pride and Prejudice*, that the division of labor between genteel women and genteel men is the source of profound and daily differences in powerlessness and power.

As in Austen, therefore, we are aware early in the novel of the traditional difference in men's and women's mobility—Graham comes and goes while Polly sits on a stool "all day long"—but we are also made to feel, as we are not in Austen, that men come and go because they have work that requires it, while genteel dependent women sit on a stool all day long because there is little else that they are required or allowed to do (20). As in Burney and Austen, men's economic privilege in *Villette* is also a source of status and of control over women in that it gives men the means of bestowing benefits. Graham is not yet earning a living, but he does have treasures that little Polly covets, and, in his use of them as a mode of securing her attention, he anticipates the emotional control which work that pays will give him as a man: "Yes, yes; you will stay with me, I am sure. I have a pony on which you shall ride, and no end of books with pictures to show you" (15). But in *Villette* men's privilege, especially their access to work in public spheres, allows them the further status of providing women with the vicarious experience of a larger world. Graham's every entry into the Bretton household introduces the eventfulness and energy of the world outside, a world which the women of *this* interior can't even see from their windows: "The evening, by restoring Graham to the maternal roof . . . , brought us an accession of animation" (16).

Graham as well as Mr. Home deny women the right to explore this world on their own. Mr. Home warns Polly that "only great, strong people"—that is, men—are fit for travel, and Graham reenforces this message by lending her a book in which the world is described as a place full of dangers for women—wild men with scarcely any clothes on, wild horses, and a goblin which might "trample me down amongst the bushes, as I might tread on a grasshopper in a hayfield without knowing it" (18, 25). No wonder Polly means to postpone traveling until she is as tall as Mrs. Bretton and can command Graham's protection. In the meantime, her experience of the world is more confined than Elizabeth's, consisting only of secondhand participation in the world of males.

In *Villette,* moreover, men's access to work that pays is not just the source of power to move or power to assume control over women; it is the source of a vital autonomy—the power to define the self and to feel approved. We are made to understand that young Graham is identified by his work as a student, the mature Graham by his professional career, and we are told that both have their share of prizes or esteem. But dependent women cannot be identified by their work at all since Brontë all but omits genteel domestic labor from the novel. Indeed, no dependent woman is ever more productively employed than little Polly, in whom domestic work is seen as miniature and, therefore, as absurd: "I found her seated, like a little Odalisque, on a couch . . . She seemed happy; all her appliances for occupation were about her; the white wood work-box, a shred or two of muslin, an end or two of ribbon, collected for conversion into doll-millinery" (25). It is this division of labor between women and men that prompts women to see men as superior: Polly secures Graham a piece of cake on the grounds that "he goes to school: girls—such as me and Miss Snowe—don't need treats, but *he* would like it" (21).

Of course dependent women do labor in this novel, but it is not at anything so visible as the performance of domestic chores, for their real job is to be self-sacrificing, is to love and serve. Thus Polly entertains Graham; she soothes him; she hands him his tea; she secures him cake while she goes without. Graham, in fact, "could not be sufficiently well waited on, nor carefully enough looked after" (21). It is as if Polly had already read a spate of manuals on the true nature of woman's sphere.

It is in sacrificing herself to Graham and her father, moreover, that Polly finds what worth and identity she can feel; but to be identified through love and sacrifice in this novel is barely to be there. Polly's very self is "forgotten" in serving Graham, and "with curious readiness" she so completely adapts herself "to such themes as interested him" that "one would have thought the child had no mind or life of her own, but must necessarily live, move, and have her being in another: . . . she nestled to Graham, and seemed to feel by his feelings: to exist in his existence" (21–22).

It is Polly's immersion in an ideologically prescribed self-sacrifice and her consequent lack of autonomy which is at the root of the suffering which so permeates the Bretton chapters. For the emotionally dependent female needs men as men do not need her, and separation, loss, suffering are inevitable. Polly is separated twice from the men who sustain her sense of being, and separation, in each case, submits her to something that resembles the agonies of dying. To be divided from Graham or her father is to ask "Why hast thou forsaken me?" is to lie "mute and motionless" by Graham's foot, is to feel "in this way I cannot—cannot live!" (19, 27). The scene in which Graham sits "wholly unconscious" of Polly, pushing her with his "restless foot" while she lies on the floor softly caressing his shoe, is one of the more painful scenes in literature (27).

One further consequence of Polly's immersion in self-sacrifice is not only that it submits her to pain but that it enforces her low status and lack of power in relation to Graham. Graham, of course, is perfectly content to let her wait on him and is fond of treating her as a kind of serving maid, asking her to "bring me something particularly nice; that's a kind little woman" or "promising that, when he had a house of his own, she should be his housekeeper, and perhaps—if she showed any culinary genius—his cook" (20). Lucky Polly. But while men like Graham may enjoy being served, may adore being worshiped, at base they view women who do both as inferior, less fully human than themselves, and naturally more subject to control.

This attitude was conventionally buried in midnineteenth-century life by an ideology which assured women of the middle class that they were both superior to men and mysteriously more powerful as well, but the contradictions between this ideology and the realities of status and power are writ large in Graham's first encounter with Polly Home. The encounter begins playfully with an homage that is patently insincere—"Miss Home . . . Your slave, John Graham Bretton"—and ends with a display of Graham's control that effectively reduces Polly to the less than human (15). Even Polly protests after Graham casually lifts her over his head with one hand: "I wonder what you would think of me if I were to treat you in that way, lifting you with my hand . . . as Warren lifts the little cat" (16).

The Miss Marchmont episode repeats on an adult scale, but with little essential variation, the elements first broached in the relation of Polly and Graham. Once again there is the "handsome residence," the quiet interior of the leisured genteel woman (30). But once again the ground note of this quiet interior is that of suffering, and the suffering is linked with a lack of autonomy, with emotional dependence on a man: Maria Marchmont has mourned the death of her fiancé for thirty years, and that grief—since she has been a cripple for the last two decades—has been quite literally paralyzing. Like little Polly's, Maria Marchmont's dependence and emotional powerlessness are indirectly connected with the division between women's and men's spheres, for our only view of her past reminds us of that traditional division between action and inaction in the lives of genteel men and women. We see Maria indoors, "dressed and decorated," sitting by the fireside to wait, while Frank, the lover, the *man*, is riding about somewhere in the world (34). Like Polly, too, Maria looks up to the man, the active one, as her superior: "O my noble Frank—my faithful Frank—my *good* Frank! so much better than myself—his standard in all things so much higher!" (33). Like Polly, in fact, she sees him as a kind of god and as a giver of life itself: "You see I still think of Frank more than of God"; "while I loved, and while I was loved, what an existence I enjoyed!" (35, 33). Logically, then, deprivation of Frank means death or a deathlike existence, means "thirty years of sorrow" and "twenty years" of "impotence" as a "rheumatic cripple" (31, 30).

What Lucy feels about this, her first exposure to the lives of dependent women, is suggested obliquely at best, but Brontë does give her some ironic consciousness of the division between ideologies about women's lives and the potentially painful realities. Eight years of Lucy's own life have been full of storm and loss and suffering, yet she withholds the details, wryly permitting "the reader to picture me, for the next eight years, as a bark slumbering through halcyon weather, in a harbour still as glass—the steersman stretched on the little deck, his face up to heaven, his eyes closed: buried, if you will, in a long prayer. A great many women and girls are supposed to pass their lives something in that fashion; why not I with the rest?" (29). What Lucy suggests, of course, is that women's lives are often more troubled than they seem, but the image of women's lives as they should be, with its emphasis on idleness and inactivity, also betrays an aversion to the very ideal of woman's sphere. The image, for example, makes us feel that idleness is unnatural. It is not natural, after all, for a steersman to be inert, "buried" in a prayer, for men and steersmen in particular are supposed to be active. Even the pleasant variation of the image which follows—"Picture me then idle, basking, plump, and happy, stretched on a cushioned deck"—strikes us as wrong (30). Steersmen are supposed to steer, not bask in the sun. It is by asking us to imagine a *man* undergoing the idleness assigned to the life of a genteel woman that Brontë emphasizes the feeling that even the ideal for women is unpleasant and unnatural.

But if the ideal is unpleasant in the abstract it is much more unpleasant in the concrete, for the lives of dependent genteel women are not simply inactive, as the image suggests. They are potentially full of pain. The real image of women's life is not that of burial in a prayer or of basking in the sun but that of little Polly Home pricking her fingers and bleeding away on the handkerchief she is hemming as a "keepsake for 'papa'" (16). Lucy Snowe, of course, despite her name and her pretensions to calm, participates vicariously in Polly's suffering, and this participation subtly enforces Brontë's oblique criticism of woman's sphere. When Polly mopes, Lucy's tranquillity is broken. When Polly loses herself in her father, Lucy is oppressed by the intensity of her feelings: ". . . it was a scene of feeling too brimful, and which, because the cup did not foam up high or furiously overflow, only oppressed one the more" (12). To love Mr. Home, to love any male with Polly's self-submerging devotion, is clearly hazardous from Lucy's point of view, and Graham in particular strikes her as "an animal dangerous by nature, and but half-tamed by art" (25).[4]

Like Austen, then, Brontë evokes a causal relation between economic dependence and lack of power, but in contrast to Austen she does not subvert this relation. In *Villette,* moreover, the modes of powerlessness with which economic dependency is linked are more radical and more painful than those which we encounter in Jane Austen. Indeed, the dependent life, which in *Pride and Prejudice* constitutes the heroine's reward and which appears protectively enclosed by Pemberley at the end of the novel, reappears in *Villette* as both painful and claustrophobic. What Brontë appears to arrive at, in fact, is that to be denied work, to be dependent, is to be denied power even to define one's self, and this is to be denied a vital form of autonomy. The novel begins, therefore, by obliquely rejecting dependency, the traditional happy ending, and by rewriting a conventional fictional script: the real history of Lucy Snowe, in contrast to the histories of Elizabeth and Evelina, begins not with an entry onto the marriage mart but with an entry onto the labor market. It begins with a reordering of the priorities previously assigned to love and quest.

Of course, by covertly rejecting the traditional love and marriage plot, the opening of *Villette* strains against ideology—as it informed literature as well as life. And it is this tension with ideology which accounts for the extensive mystification in this novel. Brontë's critique of the dependent life, for example, is disguised in these opening chapters by the fact that Polly is officially a girl of seven, and Polly's unpleasant power relation with Graham is masked by the charm which Lucy Snowe attaches to this officially child-like relationship. The ideological source of Polly's role, indeed the very existence of an ideology, is also mystified by the peculiar absence of community. Elizabeth Bennet and Maggie Tulliver live in the midst of societies that are well defined; we feel the weight of their shared assumptions, the universality of their "truths." But English society in *Villette*, the society to which Lucy Snowe belongs, seems to be no society at all and seems therefore to make no demands upon the heroine. What passes for English society is a handful of characters—and peripatetic characters at that. They appear in England and then disappear, relocate, reassemble in Belgium, and seem unrelated on the whole to any larger body. This English network, moreover—the Brettons, the Homes, and Ginevra Fanshawe—is not family or even properly kin to Lucy Snowe. Their notions about women are not officially binding upon her, and their relation to her anyway is so tangential that they seldom appear to exert any influence. The second community in the novel, a community represented by Villette, is more cohesive but is also foreign, and what is foreign may be rejected. In this novel, it usually is. Villette ("small town") and Labassecour ("farmyard"), far from binding Lucy with their provincial notions about woman's fate, are generally just the locus of certain highly traditional attitudes toward genteel women which have been half consciously projected onto the Catholic and the foreign that they may be discredited by Lucy, and by Brontë too, for the benefit of an English and Protestant reader. In effect, then, *Villette* disguises the communal source and therefore the very existence of the ideology whose oppressive weight it nevertheless records.

But, if Brontë's resistance to the ideology of woman's sphere prompts her to mystify this ideology—and Lucy Snowe at times seems remarkably free of those "universal" truths which Elizabeth Bennet must overcome—her resistance also appears to generate counterlongings for what has been denied. These are longings which inform the experience of her heroine and which ultimately deform the very shape of her narrative, and they make Lucy Snowe in some ways more fiercely bound by ideology than Elizabeth Bennet. At the beginning of the novel, for example, Brontë, having obliquely exposed Lucy to some of the unnatural ideals and painful realities of a dependent woman's traditional existence—the confinement, the inactivity, the painful emotional dependency on men—having emphasized the claustrophobic quality of a woman's life without men or occupation,[5] turns around and stresses the difficulty with which any of this can be given up. Lucy does leave the quiet interiors of genteel women for a life of labor, economic independence, and self-enhancing power, but she does not leave them out of distaste for what she has observed. She leaves because she has to. Far from casting herself romantically into the arms of the unknown, she "must be goaded, driven, stung, forced to energy" (32). Indeed, so alien is the notion of leaving the genteel dependent life that the decision to seek London appears to come from some source other than herself: the aurora borealis. "Some new power it seemed to bring. I drew in energy with the keen, low breeze that blew on its path. A bold thought was sent to my mind; my mind was made strong to receive it" (36). And so foreign does the independent life appear that from the time Lucy leaves for London *every* landscape, even English landscapes, appears dark, foreign, and often sinister.

II

That Charlotte Brontë could take so critical, though finally so ambivalent, a view of the dependent life and the ideology of woman's sphere owes much to the fact that she could afford to do so, for she had a sense of option which Burney and Austen did not. For one thing, Brontë lived in an age which valorized work. The ideal of earning one's own way rather than of being born into independency, the ideology that any man *could* earn his own way, the equation of work and duty had all gained ascendancy by 1853, and they had gained ascendancy in part because men of the bourgeoisie had acquired money and status through their own labor and were gaining social and political influence as well.[6] This shift in wealth and influence is partially evoked in *Villette* by the fact that the creatures of "sunshine," the persons of highest status and greatest income, are not landed gentry as in *Evelina* or *Pride and Prejudice* but men who have essentially earned their own way (357). Mr. Home is a scientist before he becomes the Comte de Bassompierre, and John Graham Bretton is a doctor whose family fortune gets misplaced and who regains his wealth by establishing a successful practice.

Brontë's sense of option must also have been enforced by the fact that protest over the economic contradiction between middle-class men and middle-class women, especially over the plight of genteel working women, had surfaced in the 1830s and 1840s. It had become impossible to ignore the fact that, while the doors of professions and trade were opening to men of the middle class, independent women of the same class background were still confined to the totally glutted and low-status positions of teacher and governess. Protests against this inequity, demands that single women be admitted into occupations normally reserved for men, were lending new legitimacy to the idea of genteel working women, were opening new spheres of work and education, and were inevitably casting doubt upon the desirability of the leisured economically dependent life, or so literature on the "woman question" and on the status of dependent middle-class women would suggest. But, even as manuals and periodical literature of that time legitimated genteel working women,[7] they appeared compelled to defend dependency. Both suggested the consolidation of an essentially defensive ideology, an ideology which assured dependent middle-class women that they too had significant work and significant power but which restricted them to the home, identified their work with love and sacrifice, and limited their power to "influence" or their ability to manipulate and improve others.

Brontë's particular insertion into this historical situation inclined her both to reject and to embrace this ideology. Some of the circumstances of her life required her to respect the genteel working woman; her economic situation, for example, required her to tolerate the kind of drudgery which Austen could afford to dismiss with a shudder. Charlotte had to work—the career of her brother and the education of her sisters demanded it—and so she was forced to have respect for work that paid. This respect, moreover, was grounded in her social position. Patrick Brontë had worked his way up from peasantry to country clergy, and the Brontë family as a whole felt some lingering though uneasy adherence to the idea of work and rising.[8] Certainly there is genuine admiration for the independent life in Brontë's letters. In August 1850, she writes that "there is no more respectable character on this earth than an unmarried woman who makes her own way through life—without support of husband or brother."[9]

Villette, to some extent, is the story of a "respectable character," the story of an independent life. But it is in no way a simple endorsement of work and rising. For one thing, Brontë knew too well how arduous and how barren of achievement the working life could be. As governess and teacher she had to contend with children of the upper class, children who were most often spoiled and undisciplined, and she also had to contend with the lower-class labors imposed upon this teaching, the "oceans of needlework" which convinced her that her employer cared "nothing in the world about [her] except to contrive how the greatest possible quantity of labour [might] be squeezed out."[10] The salary too was miserably low (£20 a year from Mr. and Mrs. White, with £4 deducted for laundry), but most painful was the experience of being declassed and disregarded: "I see now more clearly than I ever have done before that a private governess has no existence, is not considered as a living and rational being except as connected with the wearisome duties she has to fulfill."[11] It is no wonder that as a novel about the independent life *Villette* is often bitter, for Brontë understood too well that for genteel women work might be a barrier against rather than an avenue to power.

Still, it is not the hardships of the working life which are given emphasis in *Villette,* and for the most part Brontë's ambivalence toward independence has other sources. There is, in part, some uneasiness about the idea of economic achievement in itself, for, as Terry Eagleton suggests, Brontë felt critical of the very bourgeois comforts to which she and Lucy Snowe aspired.[12] But in the novel's unflattering portraits of ambitious women there is also a very strong element of aversion to the idea of a *woman's* making her own self-interest the center of her life, some adherence to the ideology that self-sacrifice really is a woman's virtue, some lingering fear that the "selfish woman may not improperly be regarded as a monster."[13] Connected to this is Brontë's immersion in the ideological valorization of love, her longing for the love of a good man and for the identity which such a love might confer. And this longing is sustained in confusing tension with her desire for autonomy or for self-identification. As Helene Moglen has convincingly argued, Charlotte's early feelings of guilt and inadequacy prompted her to embrace the domination of her father and brother and to depend on them, as she depended in later life on Monsieur Héger, to confirm her sense of self.[14] In this way, she was particularly vulnerable to the ideology which urged middle-class women in general to submerge themselves in the lives of men because submerging self was in their nature. It is this contradiction between her desire for autonomy and her loyalty to an ideology of love and sacrifice which Brontë encounters in *Villette.*[15]

Despite Brontë's finely intuited perceptions of the pain and powerlessness which love and sacrifice entail, perceptions subtly embodied in the first three chapters, Lucy's longing for love and sacrifice continues. It is this longing above all which makes the independent life untenable in *Villette*, and it is a longing which Brontë cannot analyze because she shares it. Indeed, the very intensity of her resistance appears to generate desire for what is being resisted. It is this contradiction in Brontë which prompts her to qualify and displace her initial criticism of the dependent life by projecting it onto the figure of a child. It is this contradiction which impels her almost compulsively to examine and reexamine the dependent existence and, in the process, to disrupt the progress of her narrative, and it is this contradiction which seduces her into creating her own untenable "happy" ending. It is this contradiction, in short, which makes of *Villette* a lesson in the virulence of the enemy within and a demonstration of the fact that intuition of oppression does not make for easy protest.

III

The tension in *Villette* between resistance to ideology and counterlonging is evident, as I have noted, in the difficulty with which Lucy separates herself from the genteel but stifling interiors in the first part of the novel. The same tension shapes Brontë's management of Lucy's entry into the world of work. The chapters which deal with this entry are the most vigorous and the most exhilarating in the novel, and they mark the beginning of an autonomy (an existence!) in Lucy that we have not yet seen. Lucy, for example, appears to take on life as she draws nearer to people who are earning their way: ". . . I have seen the West-end, the parks, the fine squares; but I love the city far better. . . . The city is getting its living—the West-end but enjoying its pleasure" (41). The effect of this work environment is to make Lucy powerful, is to give her both autonomy and control. Lucy's departure for the Continent, in fact, is one of the high points of female power in *Villette*. Here we find Lucy utterly alone on a wharf at night, ordering workmen to take their hands off her and to place her trunk at her side. Then, having heard her assert herself against a "throng of watermen," we witness her gliding off in the midst of wind, rain, and "insane oaths," feeling "animated and alert" and fully ready to sail aboard *The Vivid* (42, 43). Lucy, instead of being trampled on by one of Graham's goblins, begins to experience the kinds of power usually reserved for men.

Of course the autonomy and control that Lucy feels on being plunged into the world outside, the world of men, are really momentary, only part of that happy interlude in which the world to be explored appears "like a wide dream-land, far away," and in a touch of unsubtle foreboding she spies a rainbow over the European continent and is immediately seasick (48).[16] But, short-lived as this spell of power and daring is, it is quite in conflict with a genteel woman's proper role, and Brontë herself is in such conflict that she feels called upon to apologize for and justify it to the reader. The influence of the aurora borealis, for example, which on one level suggests Lucy's difficulty in leaving what is known, functions on another level to assure the reader that Lucy is not as unfeminine and daring as she seems: reader, the aurora borealis made me do it. A "grave, judicious" Mrs. Barrett is also drummed up as a kind of role model for the reader—"grave and judicious as she was, she did not charge me with being out of my senses" (37). And then, we are assured, Lucy herself is moderate in her conscious motivations: "In going to London, I ran less risk and evinced less enterprise than the reader may think" (38). So anxious is Brontë, like Austen and Burney before her, to qualify, justify, and in part deny the power of her heroine that she also very speciously assures us that Lucy's boldness is characteristic of English women and that only foreigners would find it strange.

This same tension between enjoyment of self-enhancing power and the ideological necessity of disguising and disowning it must account for the vacillations of judgment which mark Brontë's portraits of other independent women in the world which Lucy is about to enter. Madame Beck, for example, is a vicarious quest figure, a substitute for Lucy Snowe, and an embodiment of self-enhancing power.[17] She is also a character whom Brontë treats with deep ambivalence. Beck's function as a quest figure is somewhat masked by the fact that she is "motherly" in function and appearance and by the fact that some of her powers are traditionally feminine; that is, she is manipulative and indirect: "'Surveillance,' 'espionage,'—these were her watchwords" (55, 61). But, if Madame Beck is familiar, she is also foreign; she is something other than the Miss Marchmonts and little Pollys of the world's firesides. For one thing, she has work that pays and that pays enough to be valued, and Charlotte Brontë and Lucy Snowe frankly admire both the work and the benefits: "All these premises and this garden are hers, bought with her money; she has a competency already secured for old age, and a flourishing establishment under her direction, which will furnish a career for her children" (306). Unlike Maria Marchmont and Paulina Mary, moreover, Maria Beck can find identity in her work. She *is* the "directress" of the Rue Fossette; she is a "first-rate *surveillante*," and in her capacity as both she has the power of control: "she rules all [120 pupils], together with four teachers, eight masters, six servants, and three children, managing at the same time to perfection the pupils' parents and friends" (123, 61). Control is another quality that Brontë and Lucy Snowe admire: ". . . Madame was a very great and a very capable woman. That school offered for her powers too limited a sphere; she ought to have swayed a nation: she should have been the leader of a turbulent legislative assembly" (63).

Both Beck's work and the autonomy and control it affords her account for her untraditional relation to men. Although she does allow Monsieur Paul to disobey orders, and although she is susceptible to the charm of Graham, now Dr. John, she is never tempted into real submission or dependency. In fact, when Lucy speculates about a future for Madame Beck, she imagines Dr. John in the role of dependent, a reversal of the traditional love and marriage plot: "Had she, indeed, floating visions of adopting Dr. John as a husband, taking him to her well-furnished home, endowing him with her savings . . . and making him comfortable for the rest of his life?" (86–87). When Madame Beck finds herself rejected, she does not lie at Dr. John's feet or take to her room for thirty years. She reasons with herself; she behaves "wisely," and it is her access to paid labor, at least in part, that permits her to do this: ". . . she had an important avocation, a real business to fill her time, divert her thoughts, and divide her interest" (90). More than any other quality, it is this emotional independence of men that Charlotte and Lucy admire: "Brava! once more, Madame Beck. I saw you matched against an Apollyon of a predilection; you fought a good fight, and you overcame!" (90).

From some perspectives, at least, Madame Beck is an intensely attractive woman—autonomous, achieving, controlling, and emotionally independent of men—a woman whom Lucy describes more than once as having "very good sense" and "very sound opinions" (62). And yet none of her good qualities is permitted to sit well. As in much of women's fiction, there is something wrong, something alien, about the woman who really does make self-enhancing work the center of her existence.[18] In *Villette* she is at first a "little bourgeoise," a little scheming, a little lacking in passion, and by the end of the novel she is a monster of avarice, heartlessness, and intrigue (61).

What lies behind Brontë's initial ambivalence toward Madame Beck, and behind the ultimate aberrant reduction of her to a villain, is Brontë's ambivalence toward the life of work and self-enhancing power which is the quest of Lucy Snowe; and it is not the drawbacks of that life, as Kate Millett has suggested,[19] but its very goals which give her most unease. Work that pays is certainly the key to autonomy and control in this novel, but as much as Lucy may aspire to both, as much as she may admire these self-enhancing powers in Madame Beck, they are not powers which she herself can easily embrace. To hanker after them is to desire what stands in conflict with the ideology of woman's sphere, an ideology which required the middle-class female to be self-sacrificing rather than self-interested. And for all its discomforts this is an ideology which Charlotte Brontë cannot abandon, and cannot abandon in part, it would seem, because she so deeply resists it. Try as she will, Brontë cannot approve a woman who is successful at making self-interest the center of her existence, and "interest was the master-key of Madame's nature" (63). Madame Beck, therefore, is made to suffer from a malady traditional to the independent woman in nineteenth-century fiction. She is made radically lacking in feeling and heart, and these are deficiencies which make her unattractive and unacceptable as a model for the heroine: ". . . to attempt to touch her heart was the surest way to rouse her antipathy . . . It proved to her she had no heart to be touched: it reminded her where she was impotent and dead" (63). It is still some leap from this portrait to the Madame Beck of the final chapters, to that "heartless, self-indulgent, and ignoble" villain whose "money reasons" and self-seeking are so exaggerated that she would rather destroy Monsieur Paul than allow another to have him, but the reduction of Beck to a villain is, to a great extent, a final anxious renunciation of the working life and of self-enhancing power, unredeemed by the Victorian woman's traditional virtues—by love and self-sacrifice (377, 389).

IV

Brontë's rejection of and counteradherence to the ideology of woman's sphere are further suggested in her overt criticism of and lurking admiration for Ginevra Fanshawe, a quest figure disguised as the thoughtless heroine of a love and marriage plot. The daughter of an "officer on half-pay," "well descended" but essentially middle-class, Ginevra is actually a woman who must earn her way. Ginevra, of course, plans to earn *her* fortune through conventional methods—marriage and dependency—and this obscures her relation to Madame Beck and Lucy Snowe, but Ginevra, nonetheless, in her unvarnished quest after economic gain, may still be seen as a version of the woman who makes self-interest rather than self-sacrifice the conscious center of her life.

Brontë's judgment of this quest is deeply ambivalent. On the one hand, Ginevra's nonchalance about marrying a rather elderly gentleman "with cash" is meant to be shocking, but, on the other, Ginevra, in all her money grubbing, is still an appealing and vigorous character, and it is precisely her ambition, her frank selfishness, that makes her so (47). Brontë may invite us to disapprove of Ginevra for being class-conscious and a snob, and she may invite us to agree with Lucy when Lucy castigates her for taking presents from a man she doesn't love, but she also permits Lucy to sympathize with Ginevra's economic needs and even to enjoy her vigor and honesty about her own self-serving ambition: "Ginevra ever stuck to the substantial; I always thought there was a good trading element in her composition, much as she scorned the 'bourgeoise'" (401).

For all her scolding, in fact, Lucy actually indulges Ginevra's selfishness, as if she participated in it too.[20] She stands with Ginevra in front of the mirror: "I let her selflove have its feast" (104). She gives her breakfast rolls, and she rather likes to "let her take the lion's share, whether of the white beer, the sweet wine, or the new milk" (200). Ginevra is also rather consciously admired for her attempts at autonomy, for her refusal to please men by becoming what they want her to be: "the man is too romantic and devoted, for he expects something more of me than I find it convenient to be. He thinks I am perfect . . . and it does so tire one to be goody, and to talk sense,—for he really thinks I am sensible" (78). Although we are meant to feel that Ginevra settles for too little—she should want to *be* sensible whether Dr. John thinks her so or not—Lucy almost laughs with approval at her "whimsical candour" and rather sympathizes than not with her complaint that Dr. John is always "preaching . . . always coddling and admonishing" (78, 127).

Ginevra, in fact, far from wanting to serve men, like little Polly, far from simply granting them control over her mind or feelings, is bent on having power herself. Ever practical, she opts for the only kind of control immediately available: the transient and finally illusory power of the unattainable beauty. Like Graham, Ginevra enjoys her partially imagined control; she is as "well amused" by Graham as Graham is amused by Polly, and it pleases her to feel that "I can wind him round my little finger" (74). She is also a bit sadistic, and like Graham she finds opportunities to inflict suffering; she flirts with Lucy here or de Hamal there, rejoices when she imagines having seen Graham "sulking and dying in the distance," and declares bluntly that "of course he will break his heart. I should be shocked and disappointed if he didn't" (202, 74). Once again, moreover, Lucy Snowe both criticizes Ginevra and participates in the quality about which she is implicitly critical. In the school play, for example, Lucy conspires with her to make Graham himself feel powerless: ". . . my longing was to eclipse the 'Ours': i.e. Dr. John" (121).

But Ginevra's control over Graham is transient and in part illusory, for from the beginning her power is the power of a subordinate. Graham may elevate her to the position of someone he can worship, but he is always half-aware of his own fictions. Ginevra is at once an "angel" and an inferior, a perfect lady and a greedy middle-class girl whom he plans to "mold" into something better (192). It is not surprising, then, that Graham can recover from his emotional bondage in an instant, for his bondage has been a function less of

Ginevra's control than of his own will. Graham has merely indulged himself in a courtly mood, and "the mood of one hour is sometimes the mockery of the next" (215).

Ginevra's designs, then, are not designs that Lucy can take seriously, and this is precisely what makes Ginevra so handy. For the shapes taken by her ambition, the vehicles of *her* selfishness and desire for autonomy and control, are so patently different from any which Lucy officially aspires to that Lucy can be allowed covertly to admire Ginevra, to identify with her, and to participate in her selfishness without ever being identified with her in a serious way. Ginevra provides Brontë with a safe and nonconscious mode of exploring the self-enhancing power and ambition which she cannot consciously embrace. Because Madame Beck's ambitions take a form almost identical to Lucy's—Lucy, like Beck (and Brontë herself), eventually aspires to having a school of her own—she must be carefully dissociated from Brontë's heroine and rejected, while Ginevra, who is no less ambitious or unfeeling, can be spoken of with favor to the end.

V

Despite Brontë's ambivalence toward self-enhancing power, Lucy's own attempts at acquiring it are initially as vigorous as those of Ginevra or Madame Beck, and they are seen, in the beginning at least, as energizing and as healthy. Lucy *is* confined to another interior and to women's work, but this interior is more continuously lively than those of Maria Marchmont and Polly Home, and although Lucy, like any genteel woman, is at first properly "inadventurous, unstirred by impulses of practical ambition," when challenged to do more she responds with characteristic reserves of strategy and power (65). Lucy daydreaming over silk dresses is almost instantly transformed into Miss Snowe taking "command" over a "wild herd" of schoolgirls by ripping up exam books and thrusting unruly pupils into closets (68–69). She is instantly a "good deal bent on success," and she is happier: "I felt I was getting on; not lying the stagnant prey of mould and rust, but polishing my faculties and whetting them to a keen edge with constant use" (70, 69). "Getting on" makes Lucy feel good.

But Lucy's first year as an independent woman does not culminate in satisfaction or in feeling good—it culminates in a symbolic outbreak of rebellion, the rage of rebellion turned inward in the form of illness, depression, and hysteria. The explanation, moreover, is not simply that her job is ill paid, isolated, and confined, although all are true; it is also that a familiar craving for love and sacrifice reasserts itself on every hand. Despite the autonomy, the achievement, and the control associated with her passage to Villette, Lucy arrives at no inner or outer space which is new. She leaves two male-centered interiors for a third, and within the third, an interior seething with stifled romance and sexual passion, an obsession with men like commitment to self-sacrifice returns with all the force of the repressed.

This longing for love is conveyed in the pensionnat chapters through a series of references to feminine interiors, interiors which represent Lucy's life or Lucy herself as an independent woman. Like the interiors which initially represent the lives of genteel dependent women, the interiors now representing Lucy's life become pointed in their emphasis upon confinement and upon painful and hidden desire. Among the emblems of this life, for example, is the pensionnat itself, once a convent inside which a nun sinned in passion against her vows. There is the nun herself, hiding a secret passion, and there is the nun's grave, where the nun and her passions have both been buried alive. There is also the enclosed garden of the pensionnat, where clusters of vines hang in "loving profusion," where jasmine and ivy met and "married," where Lucy herself keeps "tryste" with the rising moon and tastes one "kiss of the evening breeze" (91).

There is the alley within the garden, an alley forbidden to the nubile pupils but haunted by Lucy Snowe, and finally there is Lucy herself, with her cold name and passive exterior holding the "quick" of her nature in a "dead trance" but giving way to "craving" cries and driving nails into the head of her "longing" for "something to fetch me out of my present existence" (93).

That Lucy's hidden longings are both sexual and romantic is suggested by the sensuous imagery of the garden—trysts with the moon, kisses from the breeze—and also by the figure of the nun who has sinned against her vows. That Lucy's feelings are specifically centered on males, or that they will be, is implied by the fact that her interiors are broken in upon by male figures in pursuit of romance. The image of male intrusion is sexual, but what it suggests most directly is that men, specifically men as objects of love and romance, are impinging upon Lucy's consciousness. The suppressed love plot, in effect, inserts itself into the quest.

Thus, Lucy's alley is disturbed by a billet-doux only a few paragraphs after she describes her longing for something to take her out of her present existence. What follows the intrusion of the billet-doux is the reflection that she has not had the experience of other teachers in feeling "power to strike and to attract" the opposite sex, and what follows this reflection is Dr. John, who intrudes upon the garden and wanders through the alleys until he "penetrated at last the 'forbidden walk'" (95, 96). Dr. John leaves footprints on that walk which Lucy takes pains to erase, but, emotionally at least, they are not obliterated. When Madame Beck rifles Lucy's possessions for signs of a romantic liaison, Lucy "loverless and inexpectant of love" suffers an attack of "bitterness" and "inward tumult," of "soreness and laughter, and fire, and grief" (101, 102). Her hold upon herself as the calm, the independent Lucy Snowe is permanently in jeopardy, and the effect is both exciting and deeply unsettling—for Lucy has witnessed the pain and powerlessness of passion in Maria Marchmont and in Polly Home.

Lucy's foray into acting—the play, like everything else in this school for girls, has to do with love—clearly functions as an outlet for her conflicting responses to women's obsession with men, sex, and romance. On the one hand, her repressed sexual and romantic feelings are released for the moment in a love and marriage plot which casts her as Ginevra's foppish wooer—it is always less painful in this novel to love women than to love men. But, on the other hand, Lucy expresses rebellion against the hold that sex and romance have upon her. She wishes, for example, to strike back at Dr. John for his power over her own feelings and perhaps for his control over the feelings of women in general, so she acts as if "resolute to win and conquer" (121). But, immediately after this display of self-assertion, Lucy swears off: "the strength and longing must be put by" (121). It is not possible in the world of *Villette* to defy men's emotional control in this way—or to direct romantic and sexual feeling toward women—and having acted out a measure of resistance to men's emotional supremacy Lucy returns at once to a state of susceptibility, half participating in Ginevra's hysterical self-worship and half empathizing with Dr. John.

Thus, although it promises at first to be a novel about quest, about a life of independence and of making one's own way, *Villette* devotes much of its energy to depicting the heroine's longing for the love of a good man—and Lucy's work, we should note, is not the only thing that drives her to this. *We* may notice that she works for starvation wages in an occupation little better than that of a servant, but Lucy herself thinks very little about such matters, and Brontë simply does not draw attention to the insufficiency of Lucy's labor as a means either of financial or of personal gain. What the novel does focus upon is the persistence of a romantic and self-sacrificing ideology, an ideology all the more persistent because suppressed. And it is this ideology that makes work and independence seem inadequate: ". . . be content to labour for independence until you have proved, by winning that prize, your right to look higher. But afterwards, is there nothing more for me in life . . . Nothing, at whose feet I can willingly lay down the whole burden of human egotism, and gloriously take up the nobler charge of labouring and living for others?" (306).

In the long vacation even the meager distractions of Lucy's independent existence are suspended; "the prop of employment" is withdrawn, and the life of the demiconvent is cut off (135). But what might pass here as a nightmare of generalized loneliness—who wouldn't suffer by being shut up for several weeks with a cretin for company—seems in reality the ideological nightmare of having to do without male love. Lucy envies Madame Beck for being at a "cheerful watering-place" with her children, and Zélie for being at Paris with her relatives, but it is Ginevra to whom her thoughts turn and return, Ginevra who "seemed to me the happiest," for Ginevra is followed by "True," that is to say, by male, "Love": "I pictured her faithful hero half conscious of her coy fondness, and comforted by that consciousness: I conceived an electric chord of sympathy between them . . ." (136, 137). Ginevra, as the woman who commands male devotion, becomes for Lucy "a sort of heroine" (137).

Ironically, Lucy's attempt to deal with the agonies of her loveless lot—she tries to get away from the pensionnat to a "certain quiet hill"—takes her out of the virginal dormitory to a Catholic confessional where she encounters still another unattractive option for the genteel woman, another celibate life spent in still another interior, doing more repetitious, ill-paid women's labor (138). Had she visited Père Silas at home she might, "instead of writing this heretic narrative, be counting my beads in the cell of a certain Carmelite convent" (140–141). Here is a life of "labouring and living for others," but it is without the love of a man, and finally that is no life at all for Lucy Snowe. The long vacation ends, then, in an impasse and with symbolic death. Lucy succumbs to a wind so cold that it pierces her to the vitals and then pitches her "headlong down an abyss" (141). In the next section of the novel, Brontë removes her from the world of work and quest and in a trance of wish fulfillment and regression returns her to a familiar English interior and a familiar life, the life of love and sacrifice, the life of the genteel dependent woman.

VI

Readers of *Villette* sometimes complain that the novel is ill structured. Characters—major characters—are introduced in the opening chapters only to be mislaid for the entire first volume before being dredged up again without warning in the second and the third. This reintroduction is particularly striking because the mislaid characters are English and the site of their resurrection is Labassecour. We are not precisely expecting them, and this reconstruction of England upon foreign soil does give the novel the curious quality of moving forward and then lurching suddenly into reverse. This arrest, this reversal, of forward movement, of course, tells us something familiar about the quest of the independent woman: it is all too easy for her, spiritually at least, to give it up.

The man who seeks his fortune is also subject to reversals, to the feeling that he'd like to throw it over, but he cannot do so with the same emotional comfort. He cannot abruptly choose to go home and sit by the fire, tempting as that prospect might be, because a sense of being destined for movement must assail him as a man. The fate of the genteel independent woman, however, is that she may always return, at least in feeling, and that her failure to make it in the world will seem no failure at all but a mode of coming to her senses. Lucy's sojourn at La Terrasse begins literally with her coming to her senses, and the imagery is not of rebirth, which is a movement forward, but of reentry, reunion, and return. In her ambivalence toward a life of self-enhancing power, in her resistance and countering adherence to the ideology of woman's sphere, Brontë simply arrests the progress of her novel and restores Lucy Snowe to the familiar world of the dependent woman. Here, quest gives way to love, and like many a working woman before her Lucy takes another look at what she has been forced to do without.[21]

What is interesting about Lucy's reunion with the dependent woman's life, and with the love plot of the novel, is that the focus for the first time is upon material comfort and luxury, and this focus does not characterize the earlier Polly-Graham chapters. It is as if Lucy's encounter with the world of work and quest had made her newly sensitive to the most traditional rewards of dependency and love—economic security and comfort of a material kind. Lucy Snowe, the hard-working independent woman, accustomed to cold rooms and bare chambers, now lies in a French bed, takes tea from a silver urn, sits before English fires, and does not work, and it is all very appealing.

One effect of this focus on comfort is to bring into the foreground the material base of the traditional power relations between women and men, for like the earlier English interiors this secure world is dominated by a man: Graham has purchased the château, Graham is its master, and Lucy takes immediately to the dependent woman's traditional power relation with the male provider. Graham becomes the dispenser of benefits, a "cozy arrangement" of pillows, a tour of Villette, a night at the concert, and some easily given attention, and in return Lucy offers him a generous dose of love and sacrifice: "I kept my ear and mind in perpetual readiness . . . ; my patience was ordered to be permanently under arms, and my sympathy desired to keep its cornucopia replenished and ready for outpouring"; "he seemed to know that if he would but talk about himself, and about that in which he was most interested, my expectation would always be answered, my wish always satisfied"; "I grew almost selfish, and quite powerless to deny myself the delight of indulging his mood, and being pliant to his will" (151, 161, 165).

Unlike little Polly, however, Lucy is not entirely committed to this powerless role, and it is not merely that she knows her own playing of it must be temporary, that she feels the "shadow of the future," or that "a pink dress and black lace mantle" cannot transform her into the kind of beauty capable of holding Graham's attention (179). It is not just that she finds herself in a fairy-tale love plot. It is in part that there is something wrong with the love plot itself and that Lucy is allowed to know it. The prince, for example, is an egoist and a bit of a sadist too, and this makes love and sacrifice potentially painful. The very privilege Graham enjoys as an upper middle-class male, the privilege of access to a lucrative profession, the privilege of achieving "a world of active good," may make him strong and cheerful, but it also inclines him to elevate himself even further at the cost of those who are less privileged than himself (169). Lucy is aware that Graham feeds his masculine self-love at women's expense without care for "the price of provender" and that at the fireside there is "expressed consciousness of what he has and what he is; pleasure in homage, some recklessness in exciting, some vanity in receiving the same" (169). She is also aware that a desire for ego gratification prompts him to inflict suffering, to pocket the letter that she drops in the attic and to withhold it until he has exacted a full and tearful tribute to its importance and the importance of the writer too.

Lucy also sees that, when Graham is not exacting praise or exhibiting control over her feelings, he is often merely insensitive or uncomprehending. The privilege he enjoys gives him remarkable resilience and energy, and like many privileged people he assumes that everyone has access to the same emotional resources. Witness Graham, therefore, with his "all-sufficing strength," "bountiful cheerfulness of high and unbroken energies," blithely advising the isolated, impoverished, and classless Lucy to "*cultivate* happiness" and "a cheerful" mind while she protests silently that "happiness is not a potato" (168, 214). Witness Graham demanding to know why a plain declassed woman can't be more like a handsome upper-class man: "And why, Lucy, can't you look and feel as I do—buoyant, courageous, and fit to defy all the nuns and flirts in Christendom?" (215). Graham may exhibit "delicacy" in being wounded, but he has a privileged man's insensitivity to wounding others, and as Lucy puts it "the sympathetic faculty was not prominent in him" (163).

But Lucy's response to Graham's privilege, egoism, and control is far more charitable than one might expect, and here is another expression of Brontë's ambivalence toward the ideology of woman's sphere—and toward the divisions of money and power which it defends. Lucy, for example, does not overtly resent Graham's privileged access to money and work. Men in *Villette*, as in *Evelina* and *Pride and Prejudice* as well, are simply granted an unequal access to both. Nor does Lucy completely resent Graham's desire for ego gratification or even his power to hurt her. What she most resents is, in some ways, not the powerlessness or pain of the dependent role itself but her inability to *be* the dependent woman, the Cinderella who captures the prince's heart. This pain is directed into anger at Graham, but it is not precisely an expression of anger at his control. Lucy is less resentful of Graham when he is conscious of his control over her, when he is sadistic, than when he ignores her, and her most bitter comments have to do with his failure to pay her attention: "He did not at all guess what I felt: he did not read my eyes, or face, or gestures; though, I doubt not, all spoke" (270).

Thus the unpleasant power relations between women and men, and their economic base, are presented more overtly in this section of the novel than in the Polly-Graham chapters, where they are masked by the fact that Polly is still a child. But overt as the oppressions of these power relations are, and as closely as she explores them in Lucy Snowe, Brontë still cannot criticize the dependent role without ambivalence and disguise. Ultimately, unable either to embrace or to reject the dependent role, she attempts to reconcile contradiction by projecting all resentment of the inequities of gender onto disapproval of Graham's class feeling and bourgeois materialism.[22] This is at once a more familiar and a less threatening focus: "Had Lucy been intrinsically the same, but possessing the additional advantages of wealth and station, would your manner to her, your value for her have been quite what they actually were?" (268).

Brontë's contradictory relation to the ideology of woman's sphere is also evident in her judgments of Louisa Bretton and Polly, now Paulina, Home. In some measure these women are attractive. In fact, for the first time in the novel, during Lucy's stay at La Terrasse, we see at length a dependent woman who seems satisfied and at peace. In contrast to the oversensitive Polly Home or the remorseful Maria Marchmont, Mrs. Bretton suggests all that is healthy and untroubled. She is a "hale, serene nature," a "summer day," a "stately ship, cruising safe on smooth seas" (155). Still, the attractiveness of Louisa's situation is qualified for the reader by a power relation that is by now entirely familiar. It is Graham who provides the house and all its comforts, who supplies vicarious contact with the larger world, who affords in effect his mother's life: ". . . at night he still comes home to me in such kindly, pleasant mood, that, really, I seem to live in a sort of moral antipodes, and on these January evenings my day rises when other people's night sets in" (233). It is Graham, therefore, who has emotional control, and Graham, for his part, rather sadistically enjoys it: "All of a sudden, when you think you are most secure, I shall go forth like Jacob or Esau, or any other patriarch, and take me a wife: . . . Mamma, she would fill your blue chair so admirably!" (181).

Paulina Mary, like Louisa Bretton, is also engaged in an entirely familiar power relation with the man on whom she is dependent, and it is at this point in the novel that Brontë suggests overtly what has been latent in the early chapters: the child Polly Home has been acting out the role that will be hers as an officially adult woman. Her role is to love and sacrifice to men who act as givers of material and emotional benefits. In Paulina Mary this traditional role is seen clearly, for the first time, as a barrier to autonomy, adulthood, and even humanity. The seventeen-year-old Paulina Mary is still waiting on papa, still thinking only of his needs, still acknowledging her willingness to do and be whatever he asks. When she dances about him and claps her hands like a "sprite," a "chamois," a "kitten," and a "child," papa looks "down on her as men *do* look on what is the apple of their eye" (239). Paulina is "nearly as much the child as she was ten years ago" and it is all charming, the object of nothing more than playful protest or concern (239).

Paulina's relation to her father is also directly compared with her relation to Graham, enforcing the parallel already implied early in the novel between the dominant-subordinate roles of parent-child and husband-wife. Although Paulina, as an heiress, scarcely needs Graham for economic survival, her relation to him as a wife promises to carry on the traditions of sacrifice and powerlessness which have characterized her relation to her father and her early relation to Graham as little Polly. Graham, in fact, is most pleased with her when she regresses, which is often. With Paulina dimpling, lisping, and forgetting to correct herself, Graham's "position seemed to become one of more pleasure to himself" (246). All that has really changed about little Polly is that she has acquired an ability sometimes to *seem* the adult that she is not. Her workbox is now inlaid with mosaic, but she retains the same "dainty mannerisms" of the child (247).

Although Graham and Paulina both are officially creatures of "sunshine," anticipating the "happiness of Heaven" here on earth, Paulina's sunshine seems lukewarm at best (368). Indeed, she is most often linked with white and winter, not with warmth or the sun, and in our last view of her she appears rather less like the sun than the moon: she is all "white and light and bridal" and her face takes its luster from Graham's (382). Paulina's fate, moreover, in pointed contrast to Ginevra's, is to disappear from the novel like the little satellite she is. The last we hear of Paulina and Graham is that *both* their son and daughters look like Graham and that *he* reared them all with "a firm hand" (369).

Paulina's vanishing act somewhat belies Lucy's insistence that she really is a creature of some substance after all, and it is Brontë's characterization of Paulina which most overtly suggests what Brontë felt the role of a dependent gentlewoman to be—one of powerlessness and dehumanization. But, once again, Brontë's resistance to the ideology of woman's sphere seems to evoke a countering adherence, and, despite her fine perceptions about sexual politics and the inequities of gender, Brontë, for the second time in the novel, displaces her veiled criticism of woman's sphere onto a form of class protest. Louisa Bretton and Paulina Home are summarily lumped with Dr. John into a single category—creatures of sunshine—and both are criticized, in the end, not because they are subordinate and half-existent but because, like Graham, they enjoy the privileges of their class.

As a creature of sunshine, Brontë implies, Louisa Bretton *cannot* understand the pain of Lucy, the pain of persons liable to go "mad from solitary confinement" (234). And it is on the grounds of her class privilege and class insensitivity that Louisa's situation in life is finally criticized in *Villette*. Lucy is made to compare herself to abandoned hermits, starving animals, and frozen dormice—all expressions chiefly of her suffering at having lost Graham's attention—and these comparisons are duly followed by a letter from Louisa Bretton in which she cheerfully tallies her own joy in Graham's comfort and blithely asserts that Lucy must have been "just as busy and happy as ourselves" (233). All this is meant to strike us as cruel in its lack of comprehension. Paulina Home is also obtuse and, despite Lucy's official admiration of her, less sympathetic than Louisa Bretton. Paulina assumes that everyone well bred must be supported in life, but she appears least to her advantage when, like Louisa, she insists that Lucy bear witness to her relationship with Graham. Paulina "showed me these letters; with something of the spoiled child's wilfulness, and of the heiress's imperiousness, she *made* me read them" (360).

Lucy's later association of Paulina with a pampered spaniel certainly enforces the element of class protest which winds like an underground marsh stream through her portrait of dependent women in this section of the novel. But ultimately this incipient protest, like the protest over woman's sphere, is never developed. In fact, protest of any kind is arrested by Lucy's counterinsistence that it is Fate or the will of God or Providence—and not the working of an inequitable social and economic system—which must account for the differences between her own life and that of Paulina: "Some lives *are* thus blessed: it is God's will" (318). Brontë's overt analysis, once again, is simply inadequate to the intensity with which she captures the experience of social and economic inequities, for we have felt the weight of class feeling and of class insensitivity in Paulina and Louisa Bretton just as we have felt the tyrannies of male supremacy in Graham.

It is not of course that Brontë did not know that systematic class and gender oppressions were at work, for in her positions as governess she experienced both with great directness. It is in part, as Carol Ohmann has argued, that Brontë's radical impulses—like her desire for power—"come into very sharp collision with the ideal of Victorian womanhood which she herself internalized."[23] The ideal required that she be accepting rather than rebellious, just as it required her to desire self-sacrifice instead of self-enhancing power. But

Brontë's protest stops short as well because it is difficult systematically to criticize what one rejects on one level and longs for on another, and Brontë harbored longings for both the bourgeois comforts of class privilege and the dependency, love, and self-sacrifice which such comforts purchased in middle-class females. The degree of her longing was commensurate, perhaps, with the degree of her rebellion.

VII

Lucy officially separates herself from a woman's proper sphere and from a love and marriage plot, for the second time in the novel, when she buries Graham's letters, and it is noteworthy that her second separation is more consciously achieved than the first: Lucy seals the letters in an airtight bottle, buries them, and then covers the hole with slate and cement. What follows this second farewell is still another excess of energy. Lucy makes a deft job of mortaring and then falls under the influence of an "electrical" mist which, like the aurora borealis, makes her strong with reinforced strength (253). And for the first time she encounters the nun—as an emblem of the isolated life—with courage and self-assertion: "If you have any errand to me, come back and deliver it" (254). Playing Cinderella has been a debilitating business, as Lucy now observes—"The Hope I am bemoaning suffered and made me suffer much"—and it is in response to her experience of genteel female dependency and self-sacrifice that she embarks on another quest plot and on another step toward self-enhancing power: acquiring a school of her own (251).

It is at this point in the novel that Brontë attempts to pair off Lucy with Monsieur Paul, and this final love plot, we should note, actually moves the quest plot forward. Instead of curtailing the powers of the heroine, as it does in *Evelina* and *Pride and Prejudice*, the final love plot in *Villette* functions as a mode of completing and justifying the life of self-enhancing power which Lucy has been aspiring to and in part rejecting throughout the novel. Thus, it carries out the revision of scripts with which *Villette* begins—that reordering of the priorities traditionally assigned to love and quest. This use of the love plot also requires a recasting of the princely hero, a recasting in which a systematic economic contradiction between middle-class men and middle-class women is firmly reconstituted as individual and is then eroded. Ultimately, the fulfillment of Lucy's quest requires no confrontation with the ideological and material restrictions of a communal order, for both have been mystified throughout the novel, and in the end both are evoked only to be defined and thereby managed as individual.

Thus, where Orville, Darcy, and Dr. John are wealthy and class-privileged, Paul is impoverished and declassed. Paul is not the best that Lucy's culture has to offer, and the very construction of his character represents a deformation of the traditional love and marriage plot. But the degree to which he is deficient by the conventions of a love and marriage plot is the degree to which he is efficient by the standards of Lucy's quest. Paul's impoverishment and declassment, for example, alter the traditional power balance between middle-class man and middle-class woman and between conventional heroine and hero. Paul, since he lacks Graham's money and class position, lacks Graham's ease in assuming control over women. We are allowed to see the effort that goes into this attempt at domination, and this effort encourages us, as it encourages Lucy, to entertain an essentially patronizing attitude toward him: "I knew that it was his love of display and authority which had brought him there—a love not offensive, only because so naïve" (182). Rather than giving him control over Lucy, Paul's class position, his economic situation, and his looks and temperament as well tend to identify him with her. Paul, in fact, is a kind of double for Lucy Snowe, and this identification between hero and heroine is allowed to outweigh the very real privilege and power he enjoys as a male—for poor, declassed, and struggling as he may be, Paul has a better job, more money, more status, more control, and a greater scope for achievement than does Lucy Snowe.[24]

Paul is also stripped of ideological support in his attempts to dominate Lucy, for the fact that he is foreign and Catholic rather than British and Protestant—like Orville, Darcy, and Dr. John—undermines the validity of his traditional attitudes toward women and the effectiveness of his efforts to control them. Once again, of course, a communal or systematic force—in this case that of ideology—is reconstituted in the hero as individual and idiosyncratic. Ideology, in effect, is recast in a form which allows it to be managed. Thus when Paul, as a Catholic and a foreigner, fulminates against Lucy for unfeminine ambition and power, when he throws barriers in the way of her progress, the effect is only to endorse what ambition and power Lucy does have and to absolve her of selfishness: ". . . his injustice stirred in me ambitious wishes—it imparted a strong stimulus—it gave wings to aspiration. . . . Whatever my powers—feminine or the contrary—God had given them, and I felt resolute to be ashamed of no faculty of His bestowal" (298). Ultimately, this ideological barrier, which has been displaced from the communal to the individual, is displaced once again. An ideological struggle between female and male becomes a religious war. Lucy's desire for self-enhancing power is identified as an expression of her "terrible, proud" Protestantism, and Paul, in the guise of religious toleration, is allowed to grant her her way (353).

Charlotte Brontë's manipulation of the love plot for the purposes of quest involves a diminution of the hero's traditional privileges and, in the process, a reduction to the individual of the material and ideological forces which have operated in a systematic, if mystified, way throughout the novel. But this revision of fictional scripts involves more than a denial of the hero's traditional resources. It involves a reharnessing of them for the purposes of Lucy's quest: Paul is not only ineffective in controlling Lucy Snowe, he is made to validate her quest and to help her on her way. At the end of the novel, for example, Brontë makes use of a standard love and fairy-tale device: she erects barriers to the happiness of her lovers and allows the hero, in coming to the rescue, to demonstrate both love and power. Paul's intervention on behalf of Lucy is certainly reminiscent of Lord Orville's on behalf of Evelina or of Darcy's on behalf of Elizabeth's errant sister—yet the barriers between Paul and Lucy take a puzzling form. Madame Beck, Père Silas, and Madame Walravens—suddenly endowed with a rampant selfishness and materialism not before noted as a feature of their makeup—are abruptly posed as obstructions to the union of the lovers. The barriers are so unexpected and so grotesque—a middle-class woman, an aging priest, and a landed crone—that they call their own significance into question, and, on a closer look, the barriers to love take the shape of barriers to quest.

On one level, what Brontë betrays here by drumming up this "secret junta" of "self-seekers" as barriers to the happiness of Lucy Snowe is her awareness that the haves of society and an inequitable social system really do stand in Lucy's way (388, 390). And to an extent Walravens, Silas, and Beck do allow Brontë to criticize bourgeois society for its materialism and its exclusion of the many by the few. Still, the haves of society are very curiously represented. They are not represented by a Graham Bretton or by an industrial capitalist; they are not represented by anyone actually enjoying the privileges of gender or of class at the moment Brontë wrote. In two cases the haves are dimly feudal figures who make very little sense as representatives of privilege and power in 1853. The third enemy, Madame Beck, is successful, but she is female and middle-class, and as such she is a more fitting representative of one who has had to struggle against the privileges of gender and class than of one who has enjoyed an unequal share of either. All three of these characters, moreover, are Catholic and foreign, and thus they cannot involve Brontë in any overt protest of the inequities of the British system. Once again, the social has been displaced onto the private, where it can be resolved by individual action.

But the major function of Walravens, Silas, and Beck is not to provide criticism of a social and economic system at all. It is to establish generalized emblems of self-seeking against which Paul and especially Lucy Snowe can be defined.[25] Because Walravens, Silas, and Beck are made to stand in Lucy's way, Lucy's union with Paul and with achievement may be seen as something distinct from, as something triumphant over, unfeminine selfishness and desire for gain, and this removes one of the major barriers to Brontë's acceptance of the life of work and self-enhancing power.

After Paul's rescue of Lucy, after the individual triumph over the social forces which that rescue represents, the novel closes with another moment familiar to a love and marriage plot. Paul, like Darcy before him, establishes Lucy in a new life and a new interior. This final interior is a bit of a dollhouse, in fact, but it is less luxurious, less upper-class, less claustrophobic than the other interiors we have seen. Most significantly, of course, and in marked contrast to Pemberley, it is also a place of business and it is Lucy's business at last. In this private world, Lucy is allowed to savor the fantasy of combining old and new, dependence and independence, self-sacrifice and self-enhancing power. She is allowed, that is, to combine love and quest, to be what a Victorian gentlewoman ought to be plus something more. Paul *gives* Lucy her school, but she must pay the rent from her own year's savings. She is properly self-sacrificing, but she is prosperous too: "I worked hard. I deemed myself the steward of his property, and determined, God willing, to render a good account" (414). And Lucy is deferential, but she is powerful as well: "The secret of my success did not lie so much in myself, in any endowment, any power of mine, as in a new state of circumstances . . . The spring which moved my energies lay far away beyond seas" (415).

Paul, of course, is still the giver of benefits and as such he is Lucy's "king": "royal for me had been that hand's bounty; to offer homage was both a joy and a duty" (410). But, far from objecting to this traditional power relation, Brontë approves it. Indeed, she celebrates it by surrounding it with Edenic imagery. It is not for his sexism that Paul Emanuel is drowned. He is sacrificed to Brontë's sense of possibilities. The combination of love and quest, of autonomy and subordination, of being what a woman should be and of being more, was simply too good to be true; it was a private fantasy, worked out in isolation from the forces of the larger world, and, finally, Brontë knew it.[26]

Throughout the novel, in fact, Brontë uses Edenic imagery to mark pleasant but transient interludes in Lucy's life only to counterpoint those interludes with imagery which insists that Lucy's life is really a pilgrimage—and an arduous pilgrimage at that. Social pilgrimage, not private paradise, is the real essence of existence for the genteel working woman, and Lucy's last evening with Paul in the Faubourg Clotilde is heavily endowed with images of Eden. Paul and Lucy sit outside; the gardens of the faubourg are around them; the air is mild and fresh; the roses look up at a halcyon moon; and Paul's voice blends harmoniously with the silver whisper "in which light breeze, fountain, and foliage intoned their lulling vesper" (410). The two dine innocently on chocolate and rolls and summer fruit while Lucy feels "delight inexpressible in tending" Paul (411). It is a "happy hour," an hour like a "White Angel," another happy ending, another version of the dependent life (411). "The next day—he sailed."

4. *The Mill on the Floss*

The Mill on the Floss so thoroughly evokes the reality of community, and the reality of larger forces acting upon individual lives, that it would seem to preclude *Villette*'s displacement of the social onto the individual and its attempts at private resolution of contradiction. The first few paragraphs establish the fictional community as complex, organic, and in motion, and we see that community as we never see it in *Villette*: through the eyes of a narrator who comprehends it as a whole. Here is a world in which the small social unit must be seen in relation to the large, the "trimly kept" dwelling house in relation to the town of St. Ogg's, and St. Ogg's itself in relation to distant sources of coal and fir planks and oil-bearing seed.[1] Here is a world in which the ships of commerce must be seen in relation to the pastures of a disappearing agrarian society, a world in which larger forces, like the waters of the Ripple, the Floss, and the sea, constantly "meet," "embrace," and "flow" into one another (7). To be uncomprehending of these relations and these forces is to be in peril, or so Eliot's introduction of her heroine would suggest. For Maggie Tulliver first appears to us in the figure of a little girl standing "at the edge of the water," "rapt" in the movement of an "unresting wheel," while the "rush of the water and the booming of the mill" instill "a dreamy deafness" and impose "a great curtain of sound, shutting one out from the world beyond" (8).

But, if the forces of Maggie's world seem overpowering, at least the "world beyond" is moving forward, and this motion indicates something potentially hopeful, at least for the figure dreaming at the water's edge. Hope does not lie, of course, in the unrelenting progress of the seasons or in the irresistible movements of the Ripple, the Floss, and the sea. It lies in a specific evolution of the human community, an evolution from the agrarian to the industrial, which is juxtaposed in these passages with the movements of the natural world.[2] Hope lies in the fact that the forward movement of community is humanly created. The community may seem an "outgrowth of nature," a kind of "millennial tree," but it is really a human production and, like the "fine old hall" of St. Ogg's, it tells of "the thoughts and hands of widely-sundered generations" (104). That human thoughts and human hands have shaped the community in the past means, in theory at least, that they may alter it for the better in times to come and that Maggie's lot may figure in this alteration.

Change of any kind is slow, however, in a world of so many interacting forces, and change for women in this novel not only appears less dynamic than change for men, it appears negative and, in terms of power, actually regressive. The shift from an agrarian to an industrial capitalist society, a shift which in this novel defines a major evolutionary force in human life, is presented subtly but persistently as a change which intensifies the traditional inequities in economic function, status, and power between women and men of the middle classes. What industrial capitalism means for middle-class men in this novel is, for the most part, easier access to status and power. But what it means for women of the middle stations is a decline in both. George Eliot, in effect, presents an analysis of that decline in women's economic status and power to which Burney, Austen, and Brontë have been responding—a decline evoked in their novels by the mounting seriousness with which inequities of power are regarded, by a growing consciousness of the relation between power and economic function, and by increasingly radical deformations of love and marriage plots.

In contrast to Burney, Austen, and Brontë, Eliot neither subverts nor mystifies the causal relation between power and economic function.[3] The perception that industrial capitalism opened the oyster for certain middle-class men, that it afforded them the opportunity at least for rapid accumulation of money and for acquisition of status and power, is very prominent in *The Mill on the Floss*, and the varying responses of men to the options presented by an industrial capitalist society in 1829 are one basis on which we are invited to compare and contrast all the male characters in the novel. Mr. Pullet and Mr. Glegg, for example, are introduced as men of an older nonindustrial generation, men who made their fortunes slowly. Pullet as a "gentleman farmer" is the most tied to the agrarian past, being unable to "see how a man could have any security for his money unless he turned it into land" (53, 88). He is reluctant, therefore, to have any financial dealings with Tom, a man of the industrial future. Pullet, in fact, is most inclined to identify with the smaller gentry. He is the most leisured of the Dodson husbands, apparently devoting his days to the consumption of lozenges and an occasional ride on a "low pony," and, as his appearance and his name might suggest, he exercises little power in the community: he is a "small man" with "small twinkling eyes, and thin lips," who knows nothing of politics and who pays his taxes without dreaming that the "British constitution in Church and State had a traceable origin" (79, 83, 63).

Mr. Glegg, a retired wool stapler, is also placed in the past, being one of those "industrious men of business of a former generation, who made their fortunes slowly" (109). Since the mark of this older capitalist mode is the "inalienable habit of saving, as an end in itself," Glegg neither apes the spending of the landed nor plows his fortune back into business (109). He has a "cautious liking" for Tom but, with the exception of a single prudent investment, is not eager to cash in on the "rapid money-getting" methods of the age (271, 109). Glegg *is* more dynamic than Uncle Pullet and he does take part in furthering Tom's progress—by supplying some modest capital—but he is not otherwise seen as exercising power in the community. He is a "kind-looking, white-haired old gentleman" who is content for the most part to count his wall fruit, to keep peace in the family, and to make quaint observations about the relation of natural and national events: ". . . before the burning of York Minster there had been mysterious serpentine marks on the leaves of the rose-trees, together with an unusual prevalence of slugs" (61, 108).

Mr. Tulliver, however, is distinctly a man in transition, a man attempting an uneasy conflation of old and new. On the one hand, he belongs to the past, being a small employer, the owner of a "pretty bit of land" and of a mill that has been in the family for generations (69). But he is also affected by the competitive spirit of industrial capitalist development, and economic survival has been for him what it has not been for Glegg or Pullet—a matter of struggle, of "lawsuits and arbitrations" (9). Tulliver's susceptibility to competition owes something, of course, to the Tulliver blood and to his socialization as a male, but it owes more to the fact that, as the owner of a mill, he is dependent upon water and to the fact that water in 1829 is a major source of industrial power. Tulliver is actually liable to being encroached upon, and industrialization, with its effect on the agrarian world, really has meant public roads through his meadow, dams upstream from his water-driven mill, and schemes to irrigate which "either were, or would be, or were bound to be . . . an infringement on Mr. Tulliver's legitimate share of water power" (137).

Tulliver responds to the new forces and new men of the industrial capitalist age, in part, by making Tom a new man too, and this is a defense at once against more powerful men like Wakem and against Tom himself. Although Tom's education is outmoded—it is the education of a gentleman, not a man of business—Tulliver's intentions are modern and even acute: ". . . it's an investment; Tom's eddication 'ull be so much capital to him" (64). What Tulliver lacks is wide experience of the new world and of the men who have power in it, along with a willingness to adapt and to have dealings with the enemy, and although, in contrast to Glegg and Pullet, he means to have power in his community, his continuing sense of himself is of a man overpowered by larger forces. *His* view of national affairs is that "the country would become utterly the prey of Papists and Radicals, and there would be no more chance for honest men" (67).

Mr. Deane, in contrast, is a man in tune with the future, a man "advancing in the world as rapidly as Mr. Tulliver had been going down in it" (182). His career, in fact, illustrates the dynamism of the new industrial capitalist world; it suggests the rapidity with which some men were allowed to rise and to earn their fortunes by advancing the interests of capitalist production and exchange. Beginning his career with no more schooling than "a charity boy," Deane works his way up from unloading cheeses to being a manager and finally to owning shares in Guest & Co., and "there was no knowing where a man would stop, who had got his foot into a great mill-owning, ship-owning business . . . with a banking concern attached" (203, 57).

Unlike Glegg and Pullet, Deane is eager to expand his prosperity through active investment and is inclined to view the human community in terms of opportunities for economic advance. Deane, for example, launches Tom in a career while seeing him essentially in terms of his own economic prosperity. As it turns out, Tom proves an excellent risk and Deane, pleased with his own judgment, pleased that a nephew should be "made of such good commercial stuff," helps him on, raises his salary, promotes him to buyer of "various vulgar commodities," offers him a share in the business, and ultimately installs him in the mill (270).

Deane, in contrast to Glegg and Pullet, is a man of action. But, in contrast to Tulliver, he is also flexible and accommodating. Movement and openness to innovation define his career as they define the life of the community and the nation and, although Deane is not portrayed as a man with direct power in national affairs, he *is* a force in the community and he *is* seen as one of those who are changing the nature of production and exchange:

> Somebody has said it's a fine thing to make two ears of corn grow where only one grew before; but, sir, it's a fine thing, too, to further the exchange of commodities, and bring the grains of corn to the mouths that are hungry. And that's our line of business; and I consider it as honourable a position as a man can hold, to be connected with it. (345–346)

II

Women who marry men like Deane do enjoy greater wealth than women who marry men like Glegg, but with their greater wealth they enjoy less status and power, or even influence, in relation to their husbands and their kin. Mrs. Glegg, for example, married to a man of a preindustrial generation, has a far greater sense of personal influence and importance than Mrs. Deane, who scarcely exists, and this sense of influence and importance is based on Mrs. Glegg's assessment of her economic function. In contrast to Susan Deane, Jane Glegg still adheres to the Dodson creed, which confers status upon the production and the producers of domestic goods:

> There were particular ways of doing everything in that family: particular ways of bleaching the linen, of making the cowslip wine, curing the hams, and keeping the bottled gooseberries; so that no daughter of that house could be indifferent to the privilege of having been born a Dodson. (39)

The Dodson creed, of course, is a vestige from another time, when the comfortable middle-class family was an economic unit and when women of the middle ranks had greater status as persons making visible contributions to the subsistence and income of the family. But despite the fact that the economic base of the Dodson creed has been eroded, despite the fact that she is not really recognized as *necessary* to the economic survival of her family, Mrs. Glegg continues to make her own leathery pastry and hard cheese, to sell butter and invest her own money, and to enjoy some of the status and influence which belonged to women of a former age. It is on the basis of her ability to make visible contributions to the economic well-being of her kin, for example, that Jane Glegg feels authority to exert control over certain members of her family.[4] Maggie "must respect and love her aunts as have done so much for her, and saved their money to leave to their nepheys and nieces" (187–188).

Of course, Mrs. Glegg's ability to enjoy the status which her creed confers upon women depends almost entirely on the will of Mr. Glegg, who is distinctly old-fashioned in having chosen a wife with an eye to getting something like an economic partner. Mrs. Glegg is not supposed to earn money for her husband, but she is supposed to help him conserve his, and her habit of wearing mouldy and yellow-spotted garments so as not "to wear her new things out before her old ones" is one function of this underdeveloped economic partnership (48). It is largely because *Mr.* Glegg is of a "money-getting, money-keeping turn" that he permits *Mrs.* Glegg to be so too (108). For it is Mr. Glegg who has "allowed" her to keep and invest the money which her father settled on her, and it is this money which permits her, in turn, to exert influence over her kin.

The degree to which Jane Glegg actually does have influence over husband and kin is also qualified. She does try to influence Mr. Glegg, but her tactics are more than usually feminine or indirect. In speaking her mind, for example, she resorts to the rhetoric of wifely submission or of feminine reproach: "Perhaps I'm wrong and you can teach me better";

"Don't lower yourself with using coarse language to *me*, Mr. Glegg"; "Mr. Glegg . . . if you're going to be undelicate, let me know" (111, 398). Mrs. Glegg, of course, is more forthright in attempting to influence her own kin, but it remains to be seen whether she changes anyone's behavior. Her most dramatic effect on anyone's activity is her effect on Tulliver's, and her criticism of the latter—which is largely confined to loud asides, and indirect reproach, and criticism of Bessy—prompts Tulliver to act directly counter to Mrs. Glegg's own interests. Thus Jane Glegg's *sense* of influence and personal status rather than the actuality of either one most divides her from the other Dodson sisters.

Sophy Pullet, for example, may be said to have less sense of influence than Mrs. Glegg, for she is less an economic partner with Mr. Pullet than a mode of displaying his wealth. Sister Pullet's clothing, in contrast to Sister Glegg's, is meant to display her husband's money rather than to save it, for her "architectural bonnet" and "large buckram sleeves" are purely ornamental and, most suggestively, highly restrictive as well (51). Even her domestic arts are remarkable less for being useful or economic than for being ornamental, unnecessary, or even treacherous to human comfort. One can still eat leathery pastry and hard cheese, but Sister Pullet's polished stairs are no more than "a trial by ordeal" for female visitors, while her deputy scrapers and her labyrinth of closets and keys are make-work without even a decorative function (79).

Like Sister Glegg, Sister Pullet has been "allowed" to keep and invest her own money, but, since she thinks less of her economic value to her husband, she has less conviction about the influence which economic contributions should afford her with her kin. Although she has financed half of Maggie's education, supplied her with hand-me-down clothing, and provided for both Tom and Maggie in her will, she does not dwell on her economic function as does Sister Glegg and is correspondingly less given to exerting influence over her relations. Where Sister Glegg prescribes behavior, Sister Pullet merely observes it or breaks into tears.

As the "feeblest" member of the family, so much "small-beer," Bessy Tulliver lacks the temperament for living up to the Dodson creed, but she is also married to a man who will have no part of the status or influence which the creed affords to women (40). Though Tulliver does choose Bessy because she comes from a "rare family for managing," and though Bessy herself takes pride in her cheesecakes, her beautifully laundered sheets, her pies, and her elder-flower wine—all more useful than Sister Pullet's polished stairs—neither she nor her husband regards her in the light of an economic partner (18). Tulliver's first requirement in a wife is not that she contribute to the family's survival but that she submit to his will: ". . . I picked her from her sisters o' purpose, 'cause she was a bit weak like; and I wasn't agoin' to be told the rights o' things by my own fireside" (18).

Tulliver's insistence on wifely submission is a direct reflection of his contact with and vulnerability to the newly competitive capitalist world, and his lack of success in that world, his inability to be predominant, adds particular force to his insistence on controlling and feeling superior to Bessy. She dresses to please her husband, or so her "unmatronly curls" suggest, and even her household routines are circumscribed by Tulliver's requirements (49). It is Tulliver who sets the dinner hour and determines how fine a dinner will be served, for, as Bessy explains to Sister Glegg, "he's a right to do as he likes in his own house" (50).

We are led to feel, of course, that Bessy compounds the powerlessness imposed on her as a woman and as the wife of Tulliver through a kind of natural stupidity—in thirteen years of marriage she has not even learned the traditionally feminine power of manipulating her husband and retains "in all the freshness of her early married life a facility of saying things which drove him in the opposite direction to the one she desired" (68). But Tulliver's requirements in a wife perpetuate Bessy's naturally dull wits and keep her low on the evolutionary scale. Thus both her temperament and her marriage cause her to play so passive a role in the Dodson clan, the role of petitioner and pleaser. It is a role which predates her marriage, for she had "groaned a little in her youth under the yoke of her elder sisters," but it is a role which her marriage enforces (40). For Tulliver, in contrast to Glegg and Pullet, has appropriated and spent his wife's fortune, thereby depriving her of any opportunity to make visible economic contributions to her family and to claim authority on the basis of them.

Still, for all her powerlessness, Bessy does act as a force in the novel. She is enough of a Dodson woman to act without her husband's consent, to visit Wakem, for example, and to identify herself as "Miss Elizabeth Dodson as was" (219). And, though her efforts only hasten the family disaster and she is essentially unreflecting and ineffectual, we see her in some measure as her own person. This is not the case with Mrs. Deane, who is significantly the "thinnest and sallowest of all the Miss Dodsons" and the sister least attached to the Dodson creed (55). Susan Deane is the only sister whose status depends entirely on the money and position of her husband, the only sister introduced as the merely passive recipient of her husband's wealth: ". . . Miss Susan Dodson, who was once held to have made the worst match of all the Dodson sisters, might one day ride in a better carriage, and live in a better house, even than her sister Pullet" (57).

Riding and residing are evidently Susan Deane's most independent activities, for as far as we know she has no household routines. In the Deane household even "the Dodson linen and plate were beginning to hold quite a subordinate position, as a mere supplement to the handsomer articles of the same kind, purchased in recent years" (182). Sister Deane does offer to buy some of Bessy's "best things," but she does not otherwise see herself as contributing to the economic survival of her family or her kin, and her closest approach to an economic function is described as "spurring" her husband on (185, 57).

The powerlessness which such economic dependency entails is suggested by the fact that Sister Deane not only fails to exert any influence over her kin but that she refuses even to make comments or to offer information. When she does speak, it is with an eye to pleasing her husband: "Mrs. Deane was a thin-lipped woman, who made small well-considered speeches on peculiar occasions, repeating them afterwards to her husband, and asking him if she had not spoken very properly" (183). Susan Deane, in fact, exerts so little power and has so little status of her own that even her death is almost without effect. We hear in passing that she is looking yellow and in retrospect that she has died of a liver disease. And this, it would appear, is the upper-middle-class wife of the future.

III

In *The Mill on the Floss*, then, George Eliot evokes in an analytic way the economic and social realities which Burney, Austen, and Brontë merely intuit or, more simply, respond to. She delineates a causal relation between men's and women's unequal power and the division of their economic spheres. She pointedly evokes the growing severity of those economic divisions and inequities of power, and she traces, in the history of Tom and Maggie, the ways in which those divisions are imposed by the community. That George Eliot evokes analytically what Burney, Austen, and Brontë more partially intuit may be explained in part by the development of sociology in the middle of the nineteenth century, by the "discovery of history as a process of logical evolution" with a "firm materialist bias."[5] Sociology itself, of course, springs "directly out of the critique of capitalism,"[6] out of a response to the appalling conditions of the industrial proletariat on the one side and to the increase of wealth on the other, and by 1860 the situation of women had also become a subject of sociological investigation. As an intellectual living in London, as the secret editor of the *Westminster Review,* as the close friend of two leading feminists, Barbara Bodichon and Bessie Parks, and as a woman mingling with other leading thinkers of the age, George Eliot had been immersed in a social analysis more complex, more evolutionary, and more materially based than any readily available to Austen or Brontë, who lived earlier in the century—at an earlier stage of capitalist development—who were not editors of liberal journals and who spent most of their lives in isolation from the intellectual life of London.

But her analysis of community is accompanied in this novel by a kind of corporate loyalty which attenuates the potentially radical protest to which her critical view of women's situation might otherwise lead. Despite the fineness of her analysis, despite the relation she evokes between the unequal economic functions and power of women and men, George Eliot does not invite us to object or even to feel that women in general are oppressed. Sister Glegg and Sister Pullet both feel a sense of status and influence with which they are perfectly content. If in reality they are without significant power, so for the most part are their husbands, and if they are silly and ignorant their husbands, if anything, are sillier and stupider yet. Bessy *is* put upon and brought to sorrow by Tulliver, but Eliot lays counteremphasis upon the genetic dimness of her wits, and Mrs. Deane has so marginal an existence that we know nothing of her private experience. She is the kind of woman whose unconscious oppression Charlotte Brontë examines and reexamines in *Villette,* but in *The Mill on the Floss* we scarcely glimpse her surfaces.

We do, of course, feel protest on behalf of Maggie, and, if the effect of tracing the decline in women's power—and even influence—from Mrs. Glegg to Mrs. Deane is not to make us angry for *their* sake, it is to make us anxious about Maggie's future.[7] But Maggie is the only female in the novel about whom we are really invited to feel that woman's lack of power is unnatural or oppressive, and despite the fact that she and Tom are seen as representative, as "young natures" who "have risen above the mental level of the generation before them," she remains a rare creature, not a historical type (239). Our objections on her behalf do not immediately involve us in objections on behalf of other Maggies to come. Indeed, objection even for Maggie's sake is attenuated in this novel. For while her entire history may be read, on one level, as a documentation of oppression and powerlessness, Eliot asks us on another level to value the oppressive community itself and to acquiesce in sacrificing Maggie to it. Her corporate emphasis, her awareness of what community is, is linked with loyalty to the preservation of that community from oppositional force.

The attenuation of protest in *The Mill on the Floss*, George Eliot's distance from the feminist movement, and her general political conservatism may be explained in part by the fact that she wrote during a period of Victorian prosperity and that, as Terry Eagleton puts it, the ideological matrix of her fiction was set by the "increasingly corporate character of Victorian capitalism and its political apparatus":

> Eliot's work tries to resolve structural conflict between two forms of mid-Victorian ideology, between progressively muted Romantic individualism, concerned with evolution of free spirit, and certain higher corporate ideological modes. These higher modes (essentially Feuerbachian humanism and scientific rationalism) seek to identify the immutable social laws to which Romantic individualism, if it is to avoid both ethical anarchy and social disruption, must conform.[8]

George Eliot's own success, moreover, and her happiness with George Henry Lewes were well established by the 1860s. She did not write out of the great insecurity and extreme loneliness of Charlotte Brontë, conditions which must help account for the protest inherent in the emotional tenor of *Villette*.

But her corporate loyalty, her attenuation of protest, is reinforced by the ideology of woman's sphere, which defines a woman's nature as completed in love and sacrifice. Like Brontë's, George Eliot's family life appears to have made her particularly vulnerable to this ideology. Ruby Redinger, for example, suggests that she was scarred in early life by maternal rejection and that what resulted from this early experience was a "conviction of unworthiness and [a] predisposition to self-punishment."[9] This conviction in turn produced an insatiable need for love, which led her as it led Charlotte Brontë to seek identification with her brother and, in later life, identification with such adult men as Dr. Brabant, John Chapman, and Lewes.

Eliot's brilliant resistance to ideology in her career was itself marked by further tension. Her sense of unworthiness, according to Redinger, expressed itself in the "ominous presence of some undefined inner threat, which she came to call 'egotism,'" and this egotism was to become identified with ambition and then with the self-enhancing power of achievement or success. In 1839 she writes that "I feel that my besetting sin is the one of all others most destroying . . . Ambition, a desire insatiable for the esteem of my fellow creatures." Writing fiction, therefore, and writing successful fiction, had to be justified by being "transformed into both a religion and a strict duty." "Proof that her writing was a positive contribution to society had to occur over and over."[10] In some ways, then, the very fact that George Eliot enjoyed self-enhancing power, the power of achievement in particular, must have made her vulnerable to an ideology which identified a woman's duty with self-sacrifice, sacrifice to men and, through men, to the human community. It is this tension between the desire for self-enhancing power and the ideologically influenced need for sacrifice and love which informs, on the one hand, Eliot's potentially radical analysis of Maggie's oppression by the community and, on the other, her attenuation of protest and valorization of corporate loyalty.

IV

Like *Villette, The Mill on the Floss* contains the history of a quest, but where Brontë mystifies or disguises the material and ideological barriers to self-enhancing power Eliot analyzes them. The economic restrictions on Maggie Tulliver cannot be located even for a moment in a junta of self-seeking foreigners, as are Lucy Snowe's, for they are recognized as inherent in the English community itself, and Maggie, in contrast to Lucy, cannot even appear to escape community attitudes by setting sail for Brussels, for her community is too inextricably and overtly part of her for that. In the first two books of the novel, Maggie is essentially trapped, a fact brought home to us by Eliot's analysis, and the effect is far from negative. In Eliot, at least, the forces which restrict the heroine are robbed of their mystery and of their claim to being natural.

Eliot's deliberate counterpointing of Tom's and Maggie's growing up forces upon us a number of recognitions which were only covertly available in the earlier novels. One is that the unequal divisions of economic function and power are causally related; another is that they are imposed on men and women both by the community. In *The Mill on the Floss*, for example, we are made to see overtly what we see only by implication in *Villette*: Tom, like Graham, is destined to act on the world and to earn his way, and, like Graham, he is allowed more mobility, more outlet for his animal spirits than Maggie or than Polly Home. Like his grown-up predecessors, Darcy and Graham Bretton, Tom is already in motion when we first encounter him, and two chapter headings, "Tom is expected" and "Tom comes Home," give emphasis to the usual distinction between the traveling male and the stationary female. This distinction is consciously maintained by Eliot throughout Maggie's and Tom's childhood. When Tom quarrels with Maggie for forgetting his rabbits, Maggie retires to the attic while Tom moves into the world of male companionship with Luke, walking "in and out where he pleased" (34).

That Tom is to be economically independent also requires that he be educated for achievement, which will be another form of power. In the meantime, his economic destiny as a male means that his future, in the abstract at least, is settled, and having this settled future, feeling destined to achieve, is a good part of what gives Tom, like Graham Bretton, a sense of self-identity and self-worth. This power is established by the second chapter of the novel, where he appears a more significant child than Maggie. Tom is the child about whom "Mr. Tulliver, of Dorlcote Mill, declares His Resolution," and in the third chapter he is the child about whom "Mr. Riley gives his Advice."

This self-identity and self-worth lend Tom's accomplishments, and his bad behavior too, a reassuring justification: "If Tom Tulliver whipped a gate, he was convinced, not that the whipping of gates by all boys was a justifiable act, but that he, Tom Tulliver, was justifiable in whipping that particular gate, and he wasn't going to be sorry" (59). And this self-justification, in turn, gives him a gratifying sense of authority in his judgments of and control over others: Tom had "more than the usual share of boy's justice in him,—the justice that desires to hurt culprits as much as they deserve to be hurt, and is troubled with no doubts concerning the exact amount of their deserts" (48).

From boyhood on, Tom thinks of himself as someone destined to "mastery over the inferior animals, wild and domestic, including cockchafers, neighbours' dogs, and small sisters, which in all ages has been an attribute of so much promise for the fortunes of our race," and, as Eliot explicitly suggests, it is merely a step from "mastery over the inferior animals," the smashing of earwigs, to the ruthless pursuit of economic gain (82). What we see in Tom, in fact, is an early merging of the male desire for control with a capitalist ethic of competition and survival of the strong. This is an ethic which Brontë omits, and it is a major element in making male power seem more dangerous in *The Mill on the Floss* than it appears to be in *Villette*. That we never witness Tom in the act of destroying competitors owes most to the fact that Eliot drowns him while he is still young.

Eliot is also explicit in making us feel that Tom, as a male and as a type of the new industrial capitalist man, spells trouble for women and for all those without recognized economic function and social power. For he not only lacks sympathy for the weak, he is inclined to see himself in the light of one destined by nature to destroy them. A boy who kicks his dog, taunts cripples, and is fond of animals for the purpose of throwing stones at them is not promising as a man with authority to exercise control. But he is, perhaps, even less promising as a man who aims at control and whose control is threatened. There are two occasions in the novel on which Tom suffers loss of confidence in his power, occasions on which an older and more powerful male subdues his spirit. Mr. Stelling makes him feel almost as susceptible as a girl, and Mr. Deane leaves him with "the sense that he really was very ignorant, and could do very little" (206). Tom responds on both occasions by turning on someone weaker than he, on Maggie, and ruthlessly establishing his superior power. If he is to stumble at Latin and at Euclid, then girls cannot learn them at all. And if he is ignorant in Mr. Deane's eyes then Maggie is "almost always wrong" (207). The reaction of Tom's "strong, self-asserting nature must take place somehow; and here was a case in which he could justly show himself dominant" (207).

Eliot refers to Tom as "poor Tom," and there is some basis on which the reader can agree. For Tom *is* a diminished individual; as an adult male he is a human being without sympathy, emotional richness, or charm. He is the only male in the novel who has no love relationship—his feelings for Lucy are really never established—and he shocks even Mr. Deane by announcing that work is all he really cares about. Still, charming or not, Tom has what Maggie does not, the power to survive, and that is a form of autonomy more vital than the power of self-definition which Brontë grants to Graham but denies to Paulina. Tom's mobility, his faith in his power to achieve, his ability to define himself and to feel self-worth, his pleasing sense of control all contribute to that confidence and that ability to adapt which make for steadiness in surviving young adulthood, much as they make for skill in ice skating, walking fences, or engaging in any other risky prospect. It is largely owing to this confidence and adaptability that "Tom never did the same sort of foolish things as Maggie, having a wonderful instinctive discernment of what would turn to his advantage or disadvantage" (58).

Like Tom, Maggie is also a "young and spirited animal," a "Shetland pony," a "Skye terrier," a "rough, dark, overgrown puppy" (13, 25, 55). But, in contrast, she is not allowed mobility. She is hedged in at every turn, and she is hedged in in preparation for a future that spells economic dependence and, if she is lucky, a pampered spaniellike existence similar to Paulina's. Maggie must be careful of her bonnet, of her hair, and of her clothes, which also prickle. And, when Tom is to be brought home from the academy, Maggie cannot accompany her father in the gig, it being too wet "for a little girl to go out in her best bonnet" (25).

Maggie is educated after a fashion, but, while Tom's education prepares him for the power of achievement, Maggie's prepares her for a genteel marriage like Mrs. Deane's, a marriage which precludes the achievement that comes with economically significant activity. The aimless and make-work quality of Maggie's training is suggested by the patchwork which she is required to do "like a little lady" or like Paulina

Home (13). "It's foolish work," according to Maggie, "tearing things to pieces to sew 'em together again," and in this novel, in contrast to *Villette,* we feel that women's work is something to protest, for this pointless training is imposed on a capable and lively nature (13). Maggie is "twice as cute" as Tom, loves books, and takes immediately to Latin (12). But she is not allowed to use that capacity or even to *have* it in any comfort; she is allowed nothing like Tom's self-identity and self-worth. A clever woman is "mischief" or a "nasty conceited thing," and her cleverness is not even clever: girls have "a great deal of superficial cleverness; but they couldn't go far into anything. They're quick and shallow" (12, 130, 134).

Maggie's response to these limitations upon her mobility, upon her desire to achieve, upon her self-identity and self-worth, is a very natural rebellion, but like most rebels she "rushed to her deeds with passionate impulse," and in the world of *The Mill on the Floss* passionate impulse is perilous (58). A Lucy Snowe may rush forth with some impunity; in fact, she is more likely than not to find a job or a lost friend but, given the fully realized universe of Maggie Tulliver and given the causal network which defines that universe, a disregard for consequence is almost always self-destructive. Maggie's rebellions, unlike Lucy's, are always seen as harmful if not dangerous to Maggie. In fact, they are generally directed at herself. Tom acts against others, but Maggie dips her own curls in the water, cuts her own hair, and resolves to starve her own self in the attic to make Tom sorry. Even the doll fetish which she punishes is identified with Maggie herself, for it is sometimes her child, something to be comforted and poulticed; and Cousin Lucy, whom Maggie pushes into the cow-trodden mud, is ordinarily a kind of pet to Maggie, like "a little white mouse" (89).[11]

Maggie's luckless rebellions earn her nothing but reproach, which is not at all good for her sense of worth. But then so do her attempts to be good by being clever. And even if she were capable of truly feminine behavior, like sitting on a stool "for an hour together," like Polly Home, that would still leave her "only a girl," "silly," as Tom would have it, and incapable (39, 32, 36). There is simply no way for Maggie to have much self-identity or self-worth in the world of this novel, for, like the witches tried by water, she is damned if she is and drowned if she isn't. One of her only resources is fantasy, fantasies of power and importance, the kind of fantasy which one discovers in Charlotte Brontë. But, in contrast to Brontë, Eliot is examining fantasy rather than engaging in it—in the first two books of the novel—and fantasy, like rebellion, is made to seem dangerous. In our first view of Maggie, or of someone representing her, she is "rapt" in the movement of the mill while she stands "at the edge of the water" (8). This is not a promising image, and it returns in her penchant for entering into a "little world apart from her outside every-day life" (27). The mill is such a world and her delight in it, her curiosity about the life of "lady-spiders," is juxtaposed with a reference to "uncontrollable force" (27). To take refuge in private or imaginary worlds, it is hinted here, is to put one's self at a precarious distance from the forces of the larger world. The material and ideological restrictions on Maggie Tulliver inhibit her very power to survive.

Fantasy worlds, moreover, do not correspond to expectations. Maggie's notion of life among the gypsies is essentially a fantasy of power and significance—and a rather "masculine" fantasy at that. Maggie imagines herself as someone in control, as a teacher and civilizer, instructing a dusky people in the use of washbasins and inspiring them with an interest in books. But, despite Maggie's superior class standing, the gypsies are not much more respectful of, or inclined to be controlled by, clever little girls than are proper citizens of the middle class. Maggie is of passing interest for her bonnet and her frock and the contents of her pocket. She is of interest, that is, for her paltry economic value. But her sojourn among the gypsies ends, predictably enough, in confirmation not of her power but of her powerlessness— ". . . she felt quite weak among them" (99). Maggie's sojourn leaves her anxiously longing for some man—her father or Jack the Giant-killer or Mr. Great-heart or Saint George—to save her, and here in this dependence upon men lies the most damaging restriction on Maggie's quest.

V

It is in Maggie's adolescence that the quest plot gives way to love, but in contrast to *Villette*, where love plots simply impose themselves on quest as an expression of Brontë's own ambivalence, in *The Mill on the Floss* Eliot appears purposely to demonstrate how an oppressive lack of options actually deforms one into the other. And in the process she delineates what Brontë disguises: the material and ideological sources of dependency on men. Eliot makes clear, for example, that Maggie's resistance to the powerlessness and insignificance of the feminine role, her rebellions against it, and her fantasies of power cut her off from the affection and approval of women, for it is the role of women in the novel, as in life, to impose on female children the very restrictions against which Maggie most rebels. The Dodson aunts, in their horror at her recalcitrance, can give her no words of approval until she is in her teens, and her mother finds her for the most part an embarrassment and a burden: ". . . it seems hard as I should have but one gell, an' her so comical" (12). No wonder, then, that Maggie turns to her father and to Tom, and finally to men in general, for love and for guidance in her quest for power. Male relations at least have less personal stock in imposing the finer points of feminine behavior, and in Maggie's childhood they are less disturbed than her female relations by her rebellious actions.

Men, of course, because of their material and ideological privileges, are also superior in Maggie's eyes, and their good opinion must count for more than the good opinion of women.

Eliot tells us that Maggie is in "awe of Tom's superiority" and that she thinks his knowledge of worms and fish, birds and padlocks, "very wonderful,—much more difficult than remembering what was in the books" (36). It is through men, moreover, that Maggie has access to that "superior" and certainly larger and more lively world of male activity. It is with Tom that Maggie can wander along the water's edge without being scolded. It is males, finally, who have been trained to possess autonomy, achievement, and control, all powers which Maggie herself desires but which the restrictions of her life as a young female continually deny her.

In fact, while Tom's childhood prepares him to exercise power in the very specific realm of economic advance, the material and ideological restrictions on Maggie appear to deprive her of the ability even to fantasize about it on her own. In childhood, her desire for power is quite specific: she wants freedom of movement; she wants to achieve; she wants to have control and to command love. But in book 4 of the novel her desire for power is suddenly dissipated, and in place of the young Maggie's explicit longings for autonomy, achievement, and control the older Maggie longs for something which cannot be fully articulated, for "some unlearned secret of our existence," "music," "books with *more* in them," and "some explanation of this hard, real life," "something less sordid and dreary" (241, 250, 251, 252).

Even Maggie's sense of restriction is rendered abstract. In place of specific limitations, specifically realized—the necessity of protecting curls, of keeping clean and dry, of doing patchwork—we have only vague references to "little sordid tasks" or the "more oppressive emptiness of weary, joyless leisure" (251). Maggie's resistance to her mother gives way to generalized "anger and hatred towards her father and mother, who were so unlike what she would have them to be" (252). And even Tom's cruelties and Maggie's response to them grow entirely formless: "Tom . . . checked her, and met her thought or feeling always by some thwarting difference"

(252). Adolescence in this female Erbildungsroman, far from advancing Maggie in her quest for self-enhancing power, appears to dissolve it, and out of the formlessness of her desires and angers she looks with new intensity to men and masculine wisdom for direction and identity:[12] "If she had been taught 'real learning and wisdom, such as great men knew,' she thought she should have held the secrets of life" (251).

Like Brontë, Eliot appears to investigate and to reinvestigate a series of dependent roles, as if exploring the options open to her heroine. Thus, Maggie progresses from seeking "masculine wisdom" in Latin and Euclid to seeking guidance from Thomas à Kempis to finding a "world" in Philip Wakem and a "paradise" with Stephen Guest (294, 394). But, in contrast to Brontë, Eliot never does find a dependent role which will do. Indeed, the satisfactions which men and masculine wisdom offer Maggie are increasingly impoverished, and they are impoverished in large part, Eliot implies, because of men's economic and ideologically based need to dominate in both the private and the public spheres. Tulliver, for example, although he continues to love his "little wench," is so entirely devoted to thoughts of revenge and to efforts at restoring public dominance that he can give Maggie no sign of his feelings, and Tom, who has been an uneven source of love at best, is equally absorbed in "ambitious resistance to Misfortune" (245, 242).

Philip Wakem, although the most gentle and affectionate male in the novel, must be predominant too. He admires and loves Maggie but, as Eliot is careful to indicate, *his* needs come first, and it is Maggie's function to fill them: "I am not happy . . . I should be contented to live, if you would let me see you sometimes" (264). Philip's need for Maggie and her contribution to *his* life are well defined, but his contribution to *her* life is largely unrealized. We hear of talk and books and feeling, and Philip does persuade her to give up her "narrow self-delusive" asceticism, but the most concrete evidence of Maggie's satisfaction in all this is that she appears once with an eager look in her eyes and a smile hovering on her lips (286). Otherwise the emotional, intellectual, and certainly the sexual content of Philip and Maggie's year together is denied or kept offstage.

Stephen Guest, of course, from a conventional love plot point of view, is the best that Maggie's culture has to offer. He is the prince—rich, newly upper-class, handsome, sexual, educated, and cultured. He belongs to the long tradition of Lord Orvilles, Darcys, and Dr. Johns. He is also an unrelieved egoist, a sexist, and a fairly trivial human being. More than Dr. John, in fact, Stephen is, on one level, a stinging comment on the genteel woman's traditional destiny, and Maggie's "Great Temptation" is an explosion of the traditional love and marriage plot. Stephen's easy authority over women, like Tom's more difficult predominance, is overtly related to the growth of industrial capitalism and to the power it granted middle-class men. Where Tom must struggle to affirm his predominance among men and where he is blunt about his assumed superiority to women, however, Stephen, as part of a newly emerging aristocracy of money, can afford to be courtly. He may find Lucy "silly" and "insipid," as she suspects, but he can afford to call her "charming" (317). He may believe that the "whole duty of woman" lies in service to a man, but he can maintain that he lives only *for* Maggie (320). He may, in fact, patronize Lucy while sitting at her feet, for as Eliot points out it is possible for women to be both "worshipped and looked down upon" at the same time (358).

The false Edenic imagery which Eliot associates with Maggie and Stephen's relationship is, in part, a comment on their betrayal of Lucy and Philip, but it also functions as a comment on the relationship itself, for the Eden which Stephen offers Maggie *is* illusory, not in relation to material comfort—we believe in that at least—but in relation to emotional fulfillment and to power. For Stephen, though more courtly than Tom, is no less egoistic and, from the beginning, the motive for his relation to Maggie is that she should look at him, that is, that she should pay him some attention: "'She doesn't look at me when I talk of myself,' he thought . . . 'I must try other subjects'" (331).

There is a touch, too, of the will to dominate and to compete in Stephen's pursuit of Maggie. Maggie is "sweet, strange, troublesome, adorable," but the real piquancy of this for Stephen lies in the prospect of seeing "such a creature subdued by love," love, that is, for Stephen (357). It is the threat of competition, moreover, that spurs Stephen on. When he suspects some attachment between Philip and Maggie, he feels "savage resistance, . . . a new incitement to rush towards Maggie and claim her for himself" (385).

Stephen's pursuit of Maggie is suffused with the same masculine and capitalist world view that informs the lives of men like Tulliver and Tom, and Eliot, in contrast to Brontë, neither mystifies the relation between Stephen's economic and social privilege and his domination of women nor excuses his privilege as natural. Indeed, Stephen himself is made fallaciously to equate his own desires with natural law: "We have proved that the feeling which draws us towards each other is too strong to be overcome. That natural law surmounts every other; we can't help what it clashes with"; "see how the tide is carrying us out, away from all those unnatural bonds that we have been trying to make faster round us, and trying in vain" (417, 408).

Eliot, moreover, appears to present something else which Brontë intuitively evokes, that seeking identity through men, through their guidance, approval, or love, is a mode of renouncing power. Maggie's progress from one man to another, her progress in the love plot of the novel, is marked by an increasing renunciation of autonomy—of self-direction and self-identification both. Her fantasies of *being* someone on her own, queen of the gypsies or a clever woman, give way to a deepening impulse to put herself under the direction of a man: ". . . she would go to some great man—Walter

Scott, perhaps—and tell him how wretched and how clever she was, and he would surely do something for her" (252). Walter Scott gives way to Thomas à Kempis, the "supreme Teacher" from whom Maggie wholeheartedly, though unsuccessfully, adopts self-renunciation as the very "secret of life" (254).

Next, Maggie accepts Philip's offer to be her "brother and teacher," finds "a sort of world" in his mind, and contemplates living with him and making *him* happy (288, 294).[13] And, at last, with Stephen Guest she feels the charm of being taken care of "by some one taller and stronger than herself," of being "led" and "borne along," of yielding and "leaning," and of finding self-identification in "admiring eyes" (334, 407, 401, 411, 350).[14] Thus Eliot's transformation of the love plot appears more radical than Brontë's, for it suggests the incompatibility of love and quest and, in its focus on the influence of community, on economic and ideological forces, it precludes the projection of the public onto the private and precludes the individual management of social contradiction with which *Villette* ends.

VI

Eliot's critique of dependency, of woman's proper sphere, is finally curtailed, however, and it is curtailed, like Brontë's, by her immersion in an ideology of love and sacrifice. The tension in Eliot between resistance and adherence to ideology, for example, surfaces in a curious disjunction of analysis. Initially, we are made to understand the material and ideological bases of Maggie's attraction to Stephen Guest. We are told something which *Villette* merely implies, that the heroine's "joyless days" in a "third-rate schoolroom," with "its jarring sounds and petty round of tasks," its "watery rice-pudding," and its catechism, have made her vulnerable for the first time in her existence to the delights of a "young lady's life" (326, 335, 350). The "leisure," the "unchecked enjoyment," the "new abundance of music, and lingering strolls in the sunshine, and the delicious dreaminess of gliding on the river—could hardly be without some intoxicating effect on her, after her years of privation" (350). And this young lady's life of leisure and culture is precisely the life that Stephen can supply. It is in fact the new ideal for wives of the middle and upper middle classes, an ideal which Eliot has made us feel that the economic evolution of Maggie's society is imposing.

To some extent Maggie's attraction toward Philip and Stephen is also explained by her lingering thirst for male love and admiration, a thirst which had its origin in the child who was never sufficiently loved or admired by women and only fitfully loved or admired by her father and brother.[15] Maggie's "excessive delight in admiration and acknowledged supremacy were not absent now," we are told, any more than "when she was instructing the gypsies with a view towards achieving a royal position among them . . ." (382). From this point of view, her very desire for Stephen is another mark of the "oppressive narrowness" of her experience (382).

The problem, of course, is that being admired for one's beauty is quite a different matter from being admired for one's cleverness or one's ability to rule and that what we have in Maggie is a rather sudden transition from a young woman with designs on masculine wisdom to a young woman playing Cinderella.[16] This is a transition which is never really accounted for. There is a point with Philip and then with Stephen when the Maggie of old appears, mysteriously, to have given way to a new Maggie, who gets lost "in the sense of her own beauty" and whose fantasies run not to active rule but to sitting passively with "Stephen Guest at her feet" (382).

This does not seem worthy of the Maggie we have known, and though the change is logical, as a response to cultural conditioning, it is not explained as such. Indeed, we feel a deliberate lapse here in that emphasis upon material and ideological forces which so dominates Eliot's account of Maggie's childhood, and what we might have seen as a cultural imposition upon Maggie begins to seem like something natural rather than imposed. One begins to feel, in fact, that the author herself identifies with Maggie's dependency: "There is something strangely winning to most women in that offer of the firm arm; the help is not wanted physically at that moment, but the sense of help, the presence of strength that is outside them and yet theirs, meets a continual want of the imagination" (356). Thus Eliot's adherence to an ideology which valorizes dependent love curtails her criticism of the traditional love plot hero, much as Brontë's immersion in the same ideology curtails her criticism of Dr. John, and this must explain in part why Maggie is not allowed to reject Stephen and the love plot of the novel on the grounds that Stephen and the life he offers her are inadequate to her happiness.

Eliot's ambivalence toward dependent love is also meshed in this section of the novel with her ambivalence toward self-enhancing power and sacrifice. This ambivalence is partially reflected in the fact that, while she protests Maggie's socialization to a life of idleness and nonachievement, she sets the novel in a time and place which deny her heroine the avenues to power which were open to Eliot herself and even to Brontë and Lucy Snowe. By setting her novel in a rural community and by placing it in 1829, over a decade before the plight of single middle-class working women became a subject of protest, Eliot makes Maggie's opportunities for self-enhancing power seem minimal. As a result, she can document the powerlessness and pain of Maggie's socialization to the middle-class woman's traditional, and increasingly powerless, role without openly investigating the alternatives to that role which Charlotte Brontë explores in

Villette and which George Eliot herself was living.[17] We never see Maggie, as we do Lucy Snowe, thrusting students into supply closets.

Eliot's ambivalence is also seen in her presentation of Maggie's desire for power as an adolescent. As I have noted before, we identify with Maggie as a child because the restrictions upon her are concrete, because her rebellions are focused, and because her yearnings for power are distinct. Maggie at thirteen, however, is strikingly vague in yearning and protest both, and this vagueness, which on one level seems imposed by her socialization, actually functions on another level to prevent us from sympathizing with Maggie and her quest.[18]

This reduction of sympathy, in turn, permits Eliot to censure Maggie for egoism, despite the fact that Maggie as an adolescent is no more egoistic than Maggie as a child. Her fantasies about self-enhancing power, for example, fantasies with which we are invited to sympathize early in the novel, become "illusions of self-flattery," "exaggeration and wilfulness . . . pride and impetuosity" (251, 256). We are actually invited to disapprove what we were once invited to grant our sympathy, and the effect is that the poverty of Maggie's options is all but buried in the counterinsistence that she wants too much.

Ultimately, Eliot's ambivalent relation to ideology, like Brontë's before her, produces a confusing and frustrating tension. Maggie's asceticism becomes something to be seen critically both because it is suicidally self-sacrificing and because it is not truly self-sacrificing enough: "Maggie was still panting for happiness" (255). Her relation to Philip is found wanting because it is impoverished and because she is a "divinity well pleased to be worshipped" (285). Even her relation to Stephen is taken to task, both because Stephen deprives her of power and because she fails to sacrifice herself for Lucy and Philip. Ultimately, then, this history of Maggie's impoverished options functions less as a demonstration of how little self-enhancing power her culture offers her than as an endorsement of self-sacrifice, of wanting less and putting up with even more.

This reduction of our ability to identify with Maggie's needs and her desire for power is accompanied by an attempt to give primary emphasis to the needs of the community itself. For Eliot's awareness of the community is accompanied by corporate loyalty, and both preclude Brontë's private and rebellious resolution of contradiction. We are invited, that is, to feel less about Maggie as a restricted individual and more about the requirements of the community which has restricted her. But, since this corporate emphasis is the other side of Eliot's analytical awareness of what limitations the community represents, this shift of sympathy is not an easy one to impose. We feel her uneasiness, for example, in the fact that Maggie herself is made into a mouthpiece for the author and is given speeches which, as Uli Knoepflmacher puts it, ought to "come from a ventriloquist's puppet and not [from] the rounded human being whose growth we have observed":[19]

> . . . there are things we must renounce in life; some of us must resign love. . . . I must not, cannot, seek my own happiness by sacrificing others. Love is natural; but surely pity and faithfulness and memory are natural too. And they would live in me still, and punish me if I did not obey them. I should be haunted by the suffering I had caused. (394)

As Maggie's speech suggests, her rejection of Stephen is finally valued not as a rejection of powerlessness or unhappiness for herself but as an affirmation of love and sacrifice, of ties to the past and the community. But her prosings about pity and faithfulness and her rejection of Stephen out of love and loyalty to the community are almost immediately followed by a sudden burst of anger—on the part of the narrator—at the community itself. It is as if Eliot were resisting the very shift in sympathy which she is engineering. First Tom is made cruelly to turn Maggie from the door, and then the women of the town are made to force her exile from St. Ogg's:

> The ladies of St. Ogg's . . . had their favourite abstraction, called Society, which served to make their consciences perfectly easy in doing what satisfied their own egoism,—thinking and speaking the worst of Maggie Tulliver, and turning their backs upon her. (442)

What is interesting here is that the women of St. Ogg's are made worse than Tom and receive far less sympathy. *Their* rejection of Maggie is not explained at all as a function of the narrow lives which society has imposed upon *them*. The "world's wife," in fact, is left to represent a generalized human egoism, which for reasons not stated takes a particularly virulent form in the female of the species. The absence of sympathy here, not at all characteristic of the narrator, is explained in part by Eliot's resistance to her own abandonment of Maggie. But at the same time this failure to take into account the shaping forces of women's narrow lives functions as part of Eliot's continuing shift away from an analysis of Maggie's oppressive powerlessness as a woman to an emphasis upon the needs of the community and to a demonstration of the fact that what the community in general needs is a revival of sisterly feeling and female love and sacrifice.[20]

In some respects the end of *The Mill on the Floss* is worthy of a Sarah Ellis, for Maggie's death appears to justify the ideology of love and self-sacrifice which Ellis so notably endorses.[21] Maggie drowns in an attempt to rescue Tom; Tom is influenced to be reconciled to her; and both recapture an innocence now billed as golden.[22] But this ending does not extinguish resistance to the ideology to which it also adheres. As Laura Comer Emery has so convincingly argued, the end of *The Mill on the Floss* is also a very strong expression of hidden anger, of hidden rage. Anger at Tom, for example, is expressed in the fact that he is drowned and that Maggie both rescues and triumphs over him:

> Tom, once rescued, suddenly understands what has happened to him, he is "pale . . . with a certain awe and humiliation." This represents a complete reversal of all previous confrontations between Tom and Maggie in the novel, and must be related to Maggie's long successions of humiliating experiences and to her awe of Tom. Maggie has never before been able to reverse the situation and come out on top.[23]

Maggie's rage, of course, is disguised by being projected outward onto the flood itself and onto the "floating masses" which ultimately kill Tom and Maggie both.[24]

This rage, however, is not just individual, for the flood engulfs the community itself, and in this action upon the community the end of *The Mill on the Floss* functions as an ultimate fantasy of power, a fantasy more radical than Brontë's because it is not restricted to the private sphere. Maggie does triumph over Tom; she does change his perception of what she is; but in so doing she symbolically alters the community as a whole, for Tom represents the essence of what is destructive of women's power and status in a patriarchal, industrial capitalist society. Eliot's corporate focus, first expressed in her awareness of the community and its forces, then in her allegiance to the community over individual protest, is also ultimately expressed in a vision of radical community change. Maggie, through the love and self-sacrifice born of powerlessness and oppression, destroys—and in destroying transforms—the patriarchal and capitalist order: "It came with so overpowering a force,—it was such a new revelation to his spirit, of the depths of life that had lain beyond his vision, which he had fancied so keen and clear,—that he was unable to ask a question" (455).

It is a testament to the deforming thrust of ideology that so forceful a woman as George Eliot should bury the power of her heroine so deeply, but it is also a testament to the degree of her resistance that she should encode, in a gesture of self-sacrificing influence, an expression of power. This power, of course, can be exercised only when the entire social order is dissolved, and its expression is ended by the huge fragments of "wooden machinery" which overturn Tom and Maggie's boat and which symbolize the real economic and social forces which have made Tom and Maggie both what they have been (456). But Eliot fills this vacant space, this momentary distance from the forces which have empowered Tom and disempowered Maggie, with a fantasy of radical action upon the world and of radical community change. And such fantasy resolutions are not to be ignored. If they are in some measure an inducement to reconciliation, if they cannot touch the material base of power divisions in one's world, they, like utopias, may still express criticism of bourgeois society; they may still express a "deeply felt need to go beyond the mere affirmation of existing conditions."[25] Such fantasies may enable the artist to "portray the present age truthfully without giving way to despair."[26] They may be expressions, however disguised, of resistance to dominant values, of structures of feeling which "however clearly affected by hegemonic limits and pressures are at least significant breaks beyond them."[27] Such fantasies become part of our heritage and live on—perhaps to be unmasked, perhaps to be more fully potent—in our own time.

Afterword

Women's Politics and "Woman's Sphere"

Examples of women who gained power within their own sphere by capitalizing on their superiority in moral and cultural realms illustrate the difficulties to come from expecting historical change through the liabilities of women's subjection. Sentimental novelists, motherly reformers, and feminine business keepers obviously exerted greater power than their immediate predecessors enjoyed under the constraints of "true womanhood." They may in fact have opened new avenues to social power through the back door of acting very "female." But the experience of twentieth-century women, suffering under a resurgence of femininity, belies the assertion that women thereby transformed the dimensions of sexual differentiation or the repressive demands of monopoly capital.

—Ann D. Gordon, Mari Jo Buhle, Nancy Schrom Dye,
"The Problem of Women's History," 1976

The process of "shattering the hierarchy of sex" remains far from complete today in no small measure because nineteenth-century feminism was hampered as much as enhanced by the belief that women, because of their separate sphere and their isolation from the marketplace, were morally superior to men and therefore society's saviors.

—Sarah Stage,
"Women's History and 'Woman's Sphere':
Major Works of the 1970s," 1980

The Mill on the Floss suggests the lines along which radical, though finally ambivalent, resistance to an ideology of love, self-sacrifice, and influence might become resistance to the economic divisions of men's and women's lives and a partial critique of industrial capitalist development itself. It is the nexus between these lines of protest that explains, at least in part, the mystification of protest in this novel, and it is the same nexus that may help explain why the women's movement as a whole found it difficult to mount a more general and more public resistance to woman's sphere.[1] Certainly feminists in Great Britain tended to confine themselves to the difficulties facing the single middle-class woman, tended to dwell upon her right to free entry into the labor market, while they refused for the most part openly to question the division of spheres itself or even the legitimacy of love, self-sacrifice, and influence as feminine ideals. "The mass of men are intended to wrestle with the earth and its products for subsistence; the mass of women are intended to apply the fruits of that toil," writes Bessie Parks in 1865. ". . . the promoters of the cause for which I speak are generally no less afraid of the revolutionizing of our family life than those are who oppose us on the strength of this very argument," writes Josephine Butler in 1869; one threatening rock is the "growth of hardness and of selfishness among women as their lives cease to be a perpetual self-oblation and they (very properly) pursue ends of their own," writes Frances Cobbe in 1882.[2]

With their covert, ambivalent, but also passionate resistance to the ideology of woman's sphere, the novels in this study suggest that women's fiction might be further explored as the site of the feminist movement's cutting edge, as the locus of radical but private structures of feelings which were only implicit in more public struggles. The texts in this study, however, cannot claim in any simple way to be representative, even of the women who were their authors. The novels of Charlotte Brontë, for example, are a series of experiments in coming to terms, and to different terms, with the contradictions of her situation as a middle-class woman, and George Eliot's novels are another series of experiments altogether. These experiments, moreover, are not necessarily progressive, for, as Gilbert and Gubar have observed, the end of *Jane Eyre* is more optimistic than the endings of Brontë's other novels, where she is "unable clearly to envision viable solutions to the problem of patriarchal oppression." Terry Eagleton, in fact, suggests that "it is not necessarily true by any means that the works of the same author will belong to the same ideology. And even texts which do belong to the same ideology will not 'give' it in the same way."[3] This suggests the need for a continuing revision of what we see as a literary tradition among women. Specifically, it suggests the need for historically complex readings of many texts and the discovery in them of the presence or absence of structures of feeling which have already been perceived in others.

For, if resistance to ideology may be seen as an emergent structure of feeling in the fiction of some female writers, justification of that ideology may be seen as the dominant impulse in the fiction of others. Fiction which celebrates women's domestic influence, in fact, might be examined in relation to the current debate over the degree to which the ideology of woman's sphere might be said to have empowered middle-class women after all. It has been argued, for example, that the ideology of woman's sphere, along with such early reforming interpretations of women's role as that of Mary Wollstonecraft, "deplored the treatment of women as sexual objects or domestic drudges, advocated improvement in women's education, upheld models of women as responsible mothers of citizens." By stressing a difference between women and men, the ideology "got around the question of inferiority and superiority." It laid a basis upon which to claim a role in civil and public life for middle-class women, and it provided the basis of a "subculture among women that formed a source of strength and identity and afforded supportive sisterly relations," a view which implies that "the ideology's tenacity owed as much to women's motives as to the imposition of men's or society's wishes." The ideology of woman's sphere, in short, has been seen as articulating "a social power based on women's special female qualities rather than on general human rights. For women who previously held no particular avenue of power of their own . . . this represented an advance."[4]

The life and fiction of Elizabeth Gaskell, with whom I began the introduction to this book, might appear at first to support this view. Married at twenty-two, later the devoted mother of four daughters, Gaskell located herself firmly within a woman's proper sphere, and within that sphere she apparently experienced a sense of social influence—she helped Mr. Gaskell in his educational activities among the working class, and she wrote her own series of controversial "problem" novels, the money from which she turned over to her husband. Gaskell's letters, however, especially those written before the publication of *North and South*, suggest ideological discomfort, a discomfort provoked in part by her dual role as writer and as wife and mother. "*Women* must give up living an artist's life, if home duties are to be paramount," she writes in 1850. "If self is to be the end of exertions, those exertions are unholy . . . I am sometimes coward enough to wish we were back in the darkness where obedience was the only seen duty of women." *North and South*, published four years later, may be seen as Gaskell's problem novel about herself, an attempt at coming to terms with that crisis of confidence over women's work and women's power which the ideology of woman's sphere was to resolve but which Gaskell nevertheless experienced. (*North and South*, not incidentally, so plagued Gaskell with headaches and dizziness that she once referred to it as this "c——, d——, and be h—— to it story.")[5]

In its focus on the influence of a middle-class heroine, *North and South* evokes that tension over women's power which informs the other works in this study, but—in contrast especially to *Villette* and *The Mill on the Floss*—the novel sustains an essentially conservative relation to ideology. *North and South*, in fact, reads like a kindly corrective to *Villette*, a novel published one year earlier and written by a woman with whom Gaskell was already deeply in sympathy. Like Brontë, for example, Gaskell begins her novel by rejecting one version of woman's proper sphere: dependent, idle, upper-class female existence. But in *Villette*, where the inequities of power between Graham Bretton and Polly Home are implicitly tied to work that pays and where Brontë's alternative for Lucy Snowe is to make her economically independent, there is such tension with the ideology of woman's sphere that the author's rejection of the dependent life must be disguised. And it *is* disguised in the first section by the fact that the traditional life of dependent women is represented by a child of seven. *North and South*, in contrast, is overt in its criticism of idle, upper-class Edith Shaw, but it gives no prominence to the economic base of her existence. We are aware of Edith's economic dependence, now on her family and, in the future, on her husband-to-be, but the exaggerated languor of her life—she is asleep when the novel opens and scarcely rises to a higher life when awake—is made to seem a matter of temperament or of choice rather than of economic situation. Gaskell's alternative for her heroine, moreover, is traditional and noneconomic. Instead of plunging Margaret Hale into the foreign world of work, as Brontë does with Lucy Snowe, Gaskell returns her to an entirely English, entirely domestic scene—a country parsonage (shades of Haworth)—where she takes on the "important post" of an only daughter.[6]

Gaskell is also more overt than Brontë in developing her fantasy of power, for the powers which she grants Margaret Hale are far more traditional than those which Brontë grants Lucy Snowe. Lucy's powers, in fact, are traditionally masculine—she has an unusual mobility and she aspires to achievement, and economic achievement at that. But the tension which this resistance to ideology generates also means that Lucy's power must continually be excused or disguised. Throughout *Villette*, for example, her masculine independence is explained away by mystical outside influences while reflections of her own selfish and economically motivated ambitions are officially condemned, though covertly admired, in women like Madame Beck and Ginevra Fanshawe. There is little of this apology for the powers of Margaret Hale. While Brontë cautiously reassures her readers that the world of work is more enclosed than we might have thought, Gaskell gently insists that the domestic sphere is larger than we ever dreamed. It is large enough, in fact, to encompass most of the major currents and difficulties of industrial capitalist society, permitting Gaskell's heroine to discuss class struggle over tea and to avert a working-class riot while running an errand. And Margaret's power, even her power over riotous working-class men, is allowed to stand without apology or disguise, for all is done in the name of self-sacrificing influence.

In celebrating this influence, of course, Gaskell celebrates the ideology of woman's sphere. In suppressing the economic inequities of men's and women's lives (by presenting the powerlessness of an Edith Shaw as a matter of choice rather than of economic situation), and in suppressing the role of community in sustaining the separation of men's and women's spheres (Margaret, in contrast to Maggie Tulliver, has no childhood history), Gaskell presents us with a version of woman's sphere which sees it as natural and as given. The same naturalizing tendency, moreover, informs Gaskell's view of capitalist relations as a whole, for the real harshness of class division in *North and South* is not seen as the product of changeable economic relations. It is seen as the product of a transhistorical force—male temperament, men, and men of the working class as well as of the bourgeoisie. Almost all men in *North and South* see life as a form of battle. All refuse to see the other person's point of view; all are insensitive, truculent, and apt to stand on their rights. And the results are mutinies, strikes, and near riots which threaten the social fabric, break up families, and kill people—especially women. Bessy Higgins dies not only of the cotton fluff which she is forced to breathe in the mills but of anxiety over the strike which her working-class father has organized, and the laboring Boucher and his wife also die as a result of Higgins' rigidities. On the other end of the class scale, Margaret's mother goes into a decline immediately after her rebellious son participates in a mutiny, and she is finished off by the gentlemanly Mr. Hale, who insists upon moving the family to the bad air of the manufacturing North. This is the kind of male behavior which George Eliot partially articulates in Tulliver, Tom, and Stephen Guest as the product of industrial capitalism itself, but in Gaskell the shaping force of economic development is muted, and the warlike thrust of men's behavior is seen as natural—as the way men are.

Gaskell's mystification of capitalist economic relations is necessitated, moreover, by her acceptance of the ideology of woman's sphere, for if women's influence is to have any effect on the harshness of capitalist relations, as the ideology maintained, those relations must be constituted in such a way as to make them susceptible to female suasion. What is needed, therefore, to mitigate the bitterness of class divisions in *North and South* is not radical economic alteration but feminine influence—the sensitivity, self-sacrifice, and love required for domestic harmony. In contrast to the martial view of social life subscribed to by the male characters in this novel, Margaret's view of capitalist society is that it is a family or that it should be, and her achievement in the novel, in effect, is to turn a series of houses into homes—first the Hales' rural parsonage, then their rented house in industrial Milton, then the working-class lodgings of the Higginses, and ultimately the structure of capitalist society as a whole. At the end of the novel, warring males like Higgins and Thornton and, by implication—at least in the future—their two conflicting classes are neatly domesticated. Higgins, the working-class male, adopts the Bouchers' children;

and Thornton, the industrial capitalist, opens a communal kitchen for his workers.

Ironically, of course, it is Gaskell's easy sense of solution, a solution which depends on the suppression of the economic situation, which accounts for the overtness of her critique of capitalist society in the first place. Brontë, who is overwhelmed by the economic inequities between women and men and between creatures of sunshine and shadow, has no sense of easy measures to be taken. It is her deep resentment of economic inequity coupled with the absence of solution that account, in part, for the mystification of class relations in *Villette,* where money and status often seem a matter of God's providence or of luck and where social power is ascribed not to industrial capitalists or even to Graham Bretton but to anachronistic and dimly feudal figures like Madame Walravens and Père Silas, who can be more safely criticized. In *North and South*, however, we see clearly enough that a landed order has given way to a rising bourgeoisie and that the power of social control and of economic achievement belongs to industrial capitalists like Thornton. In contrast to George Eliot, moreover, Gaskell allows us to see the fatal suffering of working-class people like Bessy Higgins.

But the overtness of Gaskell's position depends nonetheless on her mystification of economic force, and her solution to the harshness of industrial capitalist society leaves its material divisions untouched. Despite the fact that we are made to *feel* class divisions, they are divisions which we are ultimately compelled to accept, and Thornton's account of capitalism as a natural and progressive force is never challenged. Since the real bitterness of industrial capitalism, moreover, lies with an enduring and seemingly natural male temperament, the novel implicitly argues for the naturalness and the importance of confining middle-class women to a woman's proper sphere. Last but not least, of course, the novel never protests the economic inequities which restricted these middle-class women to the self-sacrificing role which it implicitly recommends. In contrast to *The Mill on the Floss*, which evokes the historically negative effect of industrial capitalism on the power and status of middle-class women, industrial capitalism is seen in *North and South* as purely a boon for Gaskell's heroine. It is in her transition from the agrarian world of the South to the industrial world of the North that Margaret's sphere of influence is enlarged and the nature of her power changed, made less suppressive of self and more assertive of opinion and action.

But our sense of Margaret's power is not to last, and it is largely because the ideology of woman's sphere commits Gaskell to marriage and to economic dependence as a "happy" ending and because, in the end, the significance of economic inequities impose themselves on the novel. Although *North and South* is free of that terrible longing for male love and self-sacrifice so dominant in *Villette*—they dominate in part because Brontë tries so hard to resist them—a love plot is requisite and Margaret must marry. The love plot *is* initiated at the moment of her most dramatic exercise of power, at the high point of her quest—the ultimate fantasy of the novel being that men fall in love with women who exert moral influence upon them—but the love plot develops alongside of some assertions of Margaret's economic independence which suggest that Gaskell sensed the relations between economic inequity and inequities of power and was gearing up to meet them. As Thornton grows more deeply attached to Margaret, she is freed of family responsibilities by the death of her father, is endowed with a fortune, and is launched on a career of having her own way. Just before the proposal scene, in fact, she becomes Thornton's landlord.

Like Brontë after all, Gaskell appears to feel the weight of economic conditions and to be engineering a delicate balance of economic independence, power, and influence in the final scenes of the novel. But where Brontë, in recognition of the fact that her solution is fantasy, dissolves this balance by preserving Lucy's economic independence and drowning her prospective husband, Gaskell keeps the husband and simply draws the curtain. Secretly we know what will happen to Margaret's money and perhaps to her influence as well, for Gaskell herself felt that even with the Married Woman's Property Act "a husband can coax, wheedle, beat or tyrannize his wife out of something and no law whatever will help this that I see."[7] Ultimately, for whatever *sense* of power the ideology of woman's sphere may have lent to middle-class women, it operated to stifle them by disguising the significance of economic contradiction. This is a fact that informs *North and South*, and it is a fact which Gaskell herself appears to have experienced—for all her skepticism about the Married Woman's Property Act, at least, we know she signed the petition.

Like more rebellious works—*Villette* and *The Mill on the Floss*—*North and South* suggests what it felt like to live under a particular set of conditions, suggests the complexity with which ideology might be experienced, and suggests the necessity of examining the relation of a text not just to the ideology of woman's sphere but to the ideologies governing capitalist relations as a whole. What the novel also reveals, and this is a point for further study, are the radical limitations, politically and aesthetically as well, of a conservative relation to ideology. For if in Gaskell we feel mainly the ease and confidence of an essentially conservative relation to ideology, it is also the absence of ideological tension in this work which explains its flatness. If in Brontë and Eliot, in contrast, we feel continuing difficulty, ambivalence, and tension, if it is resistance—the desire for real power rather than ideological reconstruction of past powerlessness—which produces disjunctions of form in these novels, it is resistance which lends them their essential energy. And it is this energy, I would suggest, which makes them arresting, which makes them live with us.

Indeed it is resistance, a resistance shared covertly with the female reader, which constitutes the real sisterhood in these novels, for sisterhood as a source of emotional support or collective power is otherwise underdeveloped. Females in *Evelina* are reliable only in failing to protect or even to console each other in the face of male violation. Elizabeth's affection for Jane is outweighed by her disaffection from her mother, from Mary, Kitty, and Lydia, and by her sense of being betrayed by the marriage of her best friend. In *Villette* Lucy's subtle identification with Ginevra and Madame Beck is offset by a formal repudiation of their influence, and her admiration for Mrs. Bretton and Paulina Home must strike us as more wishful than real. In *The Mill on the Floss* Maggie is more oppressed than sustained by the female community, and even Lucy's loving gesture is followed by silence and isolation. In these novels we fail to see women united by their self-sacrificing influence, by their valorization of the heart, their freedom from carnal passion, their membership in associations, or even their consciousness of belonging to a separate sphere. Indeed sisterhood in these novels would seem to be confined to a relation between author and reader, that "covert solidarity"[8] which Elaine Showalter posits as a feature of women's literary subculture in the nineteenth century, that submerged consciousness of the fact, in writers like Brontë and Eliot in particular, that writing novels might constitute a subversive activity, an expression of solidarity with the rebellious reader, a mode of social strategy—and a form of struggle.

Notes

Preface

1. Judith Lowder Newton, "*Evelina*: or, The History of a Young Lady's Entrance into the Marriage Market," *Modern Language Studies* 6 (Spring 1976): 27–42.
2. Carolyn C. Lougee, "Modern European History," *Signs* 2 (1977): 630.
3. *Woman, Culture, and Society*, ed. Michelle Zimbalist Rosaldo and Louisa Lamphere, p. 9.
4. Barbara Bellow Watson, "On Power and the Literary Text," *Signs* 1 (1975): 113, 115. See Michel Foucault, "The State is superstructural in relation to a whole series of power networks that invest the body, sexuality, the family, kinship, knowledge, technology and so forth. True, these networks stand in a conditioning-conditioned relationship to a kind of "meta-power" which is structured essentially round a certain number of great prohibition functions; but this meta-power with its prohibitions can only take hold and secure its footing where it is rooted in a whole series of multiple and indefinite power relations that supply the necessary basis for the great negative forms of power." "Truth and Power," *Power/Knowledge: Selected Interviews and Other Writings 1972–1977*, ed. Colin Gordon, p. 122.
5. Sheila Ryan Johansson, "'Herstory' as History: A New Field or Another Fad?" in *Liberating Women's History*, ed. Berenice A. Carroll, p. 401; Gerda Lerner, "Placing Women in History: A 1975 Perspective," idem, p. 359.
6. Lougee, "Modern European History," p. 630.
7. Papers from the first conference have appeared as *Women and Men: The Consequences of Power: A Collection of New Essays*, edited by Dana V. Hiller and Robin Ann Sheets, 1977. Selected papers from the second conference have been published in *Feminist Studies* 5 (Spring 1979).
8. Patricia Spacks, *The Female Imagination*; Françoise Basch, *Relative Creatures*; Ellen Moers, *Literary Women*; Elaine

Showalter, *A Literature of Their Own*; Judith Fetterley, *The Resisting Reader*; Nina Auerbach, *Communities of Women.*

9. Watson, "Power and the Literary Text," p. 113.
10. Ellen DuBois et al., "Politics and Culture in Women's History: A Symposium," *Feminist Studies* 6 (Spring 1980): 59; Lerner, "Placing Women in History," p. 365.
11. Sarah Stage, "Women's History and 'Woman's Sphere': Major Works of the 1970s," *Socialist Review* 50/51 (March–June 1980): 246.
12. Judith Stacey, letter to author, July 7, 1980.
13. Johansson, " 'Herstory' as History," p. 401; DuBois et al., "Politics and Culture in Women's History," p. 29.
14. Auerbach, *Communities of Women*, p. 7; Terry Eagleton, *Marxism and Literary Criticism*, p. 5. Although ideology may be defined more broadly as "a representational structure which allows the individual subject to conceive or imagine his or her lived relationship to transpersonal realities such as the social structure or the collective logic of history," I use the term in this more restrictive sense throughout. Ideology may not necessarily involve miscognition but "that it does so in class society says something of the conditions necessary in such societies for securing the relative coherence of the subject." Fredric Jameson, *The Political Unconscious*, p. 30; Terry Eagleton, "Ideology, Fiction, Narrative," *Social Text* 2 (Summer 1979): 65.
15. Barbara Haber, "Is Personal Life Still a Political Issue?" *Feminist Studies* 5 (Fall 1979): 419; Florence Howe, "Women and the Power to Change," in *Women and the Power to Change*, ed. Florence Howe, pp. 129, 131.
16. Stage, "Women's History and 'Woman's Sphere,'" pp. 245–246.
17. Lillian S. Robinson, *Sex, Class, and Culture*, p. 5.
18. I am indebted here to Ros Petchesky.
19. Ann D. Gordon, Mari Jo Buhle, and Nancy Schrom Dye, "The Problem of Women's History," in *Liberating Women's History*, ed. Carroll, p. 85.
20. Fredric Jameson, *Marxism and Form*, p. 367.
21. Robinson, *Sex, Class, and Culture*, p. 45.

Introduction

1. Elizabeth Gaskell, letter to Eliza Fox, [April? 1850], letter 69, in *The Letters of Mrs. Gaskell*, ed. J. A. V. Chapple and Arthur Pollard, p. 109.

2. Frances Power Cobbe, "The Final Cause of Woman," in *Woman's Work and Woman's Culture*, ed. Josephine E. Butler, p. 1.
3. John Gregory, *A Father's Legacy to His Daughters*, pp. 6–7, 52.
4. James Fordyce, *Sermons to Young Women*, 1: 24, 26, 213.
5. Thomas Gisborne, *An Enquiry into the Duties of the Female Sex*, pp. 8, 6; Sarah Ellis, *The Women of England*, p. 6.
6. "Advice to Young Ladies on the Improvement of the Mind," *Edinburgh Review* 15 (January 1810): 314; Henry Thomas Buckle, "The Influence of Women on the Progress of Knowledge," *Fraser's Magazine* 57 (April 1858): 396, 397; "Rights and Conditions of Women," *Edinburgh Review* 73 (January 1841): 204; "Spirit of Society in England and France," *Edinburgh Review* 52 (January 1831): 378.
7. "The Female Character," *Fraser's Magazine* 7 (1833): 593; "Rights and Conditions of Women," pp. 192, 204; P.M.Y., "Woman and Her Social Position," *Westminster Review* 35 (January 1841): 22, 25.
8. Sarah Ellis, *The Wives of England*, p. 26; Ellis, *Women of England*, pp. 15–16.
9. Ellis, *Wives of England*, pp. 41, 37, 14, 46.
10. Elizabeth Janeway, "On the Power of the Weak," *Signs* 1 (1975): 105.
11. Natalie Zemon Davis, "'Women's History' in Transition: The European Case," *Feminist Studies* 3 (Spring–Summer 1976): 90.
12. Berenice A. Carroll, "Peace Research: The Cult of Power," *Journal of Conflict Resolution* 16 (December 1972): 585, 588, 589, 591.
13. Showalter, *Literature of Their Own*, pp. 19, 21, 22, 23; Sandra M. Gilbert and Susan Gubar, *The Madwoman in the Attic*, pp. 49, 51.
14. See Jean E. Kennard, *Victims of Convention*, p. 13. Much of my own thinking about love and quest plots comes from Rachel Blau DuPlessis.
15. Eagleton, *Marxism and Literary Criticism*, p. 35.
16. Raymond Williams, *Marxism and Literature*, pp. 132, 131.
17. George Eliot, *The Mill on the Floss*, ed. Gordon S. Haight, p. 304.
18. Spacks, *Female Imagination*, p. 219; Showalter, *Literature of Their Own*, p. 28; Gilbert and Gubar, *Madwoman in the Attic*, p. 73; Robinson, *Sex, Class, and Culture*, p. 80.
19. Gilbert and Gubar, *Madwoman in the Attic*, pp. xi, 49; Showalter, *Literature of Their Own*, p. 12.

20. Terry Eagleton, *Criticism and Ideology*, p. 72.
21. I am perhaps closer here to Pierre Macherey: "The literary work must be studied in a double perspective: in relation to history, and in relation to an ideological version of that history." A text, however, does not "reflect" history for Macherey but "by means of contradictory images . . . represents and evokes the historical contradictions of the period." See *A Theory of Literary Production*, trans. Geoffrey Wall, pp. 115, 126.
22. Charles E. Rosenberg, "Introduction: History and Experience," *The Family in History*, pp. 2, 3.
23. Eagleton, *Criticism and Ideology*, p. 101; Eagleton, *Marxism and Literary Criticism*, p. 18.
24. Karl Marx, "Preface," *A Contribution to the Critique of Political Economy*, quoted in *Dynamics of Social Change*, ed. Howard Selsam, David Goldway, and Harry Martel, p. 52.
25. Gregory, *Legacy*, p. 51; Fordyce, *Sermons*, p. 224; Gisborne, *Enquiry*, pp. 2, 7; Ellis, *Women of England*, pp. 5, 14.
26. Eric J. Hobsbawm, *The Age of Revolution*, pp. 226–227; see also Ivy Pinchbeck, *Women Workers and the Industrial Revolution*, pp. 314–315.
27. Eric Richards, "Women in the British Economy since about 1700: An Interpretation," *History* 59 (October 1974): 337, 349.
28. See Lee Holcombe, *Victorian Ladies at Work*, p. 216.
29. The decline of household industry and the separation of men's work from the home are well documented. See, for example, Alice Clark, *The Working Life of Women in the Seventeenth Century*, p. 269; Pinchbeck, *Women Workers and the Industrial Revolution*, p. 307; Peter Laslett, *The World We Have Lost*, p. 17; Richards, "Women in the British Economy," p. 345; Theresa M. McBride, "The Long Road Home: Women's Work and Industrialization," in *Becoming Visible*, ed. Renate Bridenthal and Claudia Koonz, p. 283.
30. See Lise Vogel, "The Contested Domain: A Note on the Family in the Transition to Capitalism," *Marxist Perspectives* 1 (Spring 1978): 63, 66. See also Nancy F. Cott, *The Bonds of Womanhood*, p. 61.
31. Patricia Branca argues persuasively that middle-class women were not idle, as women's manuals of the period often suggest, but I think it likely that manuals which were, as Branca maintains, "naggingly critical of middle-class women" reflected a general cultural tension about the recognized economic func-

tion of such women and about the status of women's work. See *Silent Sisterhood*, p. 16.

32. "Advice to Young Ladies," p. 300; P.M.Y., "Woman and Her Social Position," p. 15.
33. John Boyd-Kinnear, "The Social Position of Women in the Present Age," in *Woman's Work and Woman's Culture*, ed. Butler, pp. 334–335.
34. See Clark, *Working Life of Women*, p. 302; Pinchbeck, *Women Workers and the Industrial Revolution*, p. 312; Heidi Hartmann, "Capitalism, Patriarchy, and Job Segregation by Sex," *Signs* 1 (1976): 152; Margaret George, "From 'Goodwife' to 'Mistress': The Transformation of the Female in Bourgeois Culture," *Science and Society* 37 (1973): 156.
35. Hobsbawm, *Age of Revolution*, pp. 57, 249; Cott, *Bonds of Womanhood*, p. 70.
36. "Female Labour," *Fraser's Magazine* 61 (March 1860): 371, 370.
37. Cott, *Bonds of Womanhood*, p. 69.
38. Friedrich Engels, quoted in Macherey, *Theory of Literary Production*, p. 119.

1. *Evelina*

1. Frances Burney, letter to Thomas Lowndes, December 1776, quoted in Joyce Hemlow, *The History of Fanny Burney*, p. 65.
2. Frances Burney, *Evelina: or, The History of a Young Lady's Entrance into the World*, pp. 18, 33. Subsequent references appear in the text.
3. Hemlow, *History*, pp. 28, 35, 44.
4. Ibid., p. 108.
5. Frances Burney, *The Early Diary of Frances Burney, 1768–1778*, ed. Annie Raine Ellis, 2: 51.
6. Ibid., p. 54.
7. Ibid., pp. 51, 69.
8. Ibid., pp. 70, 74, 75.
9. Quoted in Robert Palfrey Utter and Gwendolyn Bridges Needham, *Pamela's Daughters*, p. 25.
10. Ibid., p. 33; also see Ian Watt, *The Rise of the Novel*, pp. 144–145.
11. Gregory is quoted in Utter and Needham, *Pamela's Daughters*, p. 31; Gisborne, *Enquiry*, p. 155.
12. Gisborne, *Enquiry*, pp. 171–172. See also Utter and Needham,

Pamela's Daughters, pp. 30–31, and Watt, *Rise of the Novel*, pp. 142–144.

13. Harrison R. Steeves is practically alone in noting that "London was then a scene of predatory enterprise upon women of all classes." See *Before Jane Austen*, p. 205.
14. In 1750, according to Eric Hobsbawm, the system of rural "putting out" or "domestic" industry had already tightened a web of cash transactions over England, and Whig grandees "knew quite well that the power of the country, and their own, rested on a readiness to make money militantly and commercially," but it was not until the 1780s that the "comfortable and rich classes accumulated income so fast and in such vast quantities as to exceed all available possibilities of spending and investment." See *Industry and Empire*, pp. 29, 32; *Age of Revolution*, pp. 49, 65. Walter E. Houghton suggests that money consciousness and money worship were "consequent on the great increase of business activity which accompanied the Agrarian and Industrial Revolutions" and that both "had emerged before 1830, and by then had become an established fact." See *The Victorian Frame of Mind, 1830–1870*, p. 183.
15. Marlene Legates writes that the myth has been seen as "an attempt on the part of the upper classes to consolidate their precariously won prosperity and security" against the "outs" of society and that it has also been seen as a defense of the "fully secular society with its humane and refined controls." See "The Cult of Womanhood in Eighteenth-Century Thought," *Eighteenth-Century Studies* 10 (Fall 1976): 31, 38, 24, 35.
16. John J. Richetti, *Popular Fiction before Richardson*, pp. 125, 148, 152. See also Watt, *Rise of the Novel*, p. 161. Watt suggests that the new emphasis on female sexual innocence was brought about by the "very difficulties in the situation of women."
17. Courtly feeling, according to C. S. Lewis, first arises in the courts and has been rightly described as a "feudalisation of love." The essence of the fiction, of course, is that the lady is lord, the man her vassal, but, as Leonard Foster suggests, the convention is really a literary fiction meant to compensate for a real state of affairs in which it was a man's world and a violent one at that. See Lewis' *The Allegory of Love*, pp. 13, 2, and Foster's *The Icy Fire*, p. 1.
18. Hemlow, *History*, p. 108.

19. George Eliot, *Middlemarch*, ed. Gordon S. Haight, p. 11.
20. Hemlow, *History*, p. 31.

2. *Pride and Prejudice*

1. Jane Austen, *Pride and Prejudice*, p. 36. Subsequent references appear in the text.
2. See Hobsbawm's chapter, "The Career Open to Talent," *Age of Revolution*, p. 226, and see Pinchbeck, *Women Workers and the Industrial Revolution*, p. 315.
3. Jane Austen, letter to Frank Austen, July 3, 1813, letter 8.1, in *Jane Austen's Letters to Her Sister Cassandra and Others*, ed. R. W. Chapman, p. 317.
4. Ibid., pp. 306–310, 328, 326, 321, 352, 361, 367.
5. Ibid., p. 141.
6. Douglas Bush suggests that rejected proposals "have more dramatic possibilities than happy acceptances," but the "dramatic possibilities," I feel, tend to one end—the deflation of male power. See *Jane Austen*, p. 95.
7. Critics such as Frank W. Bradbrook and Kenneth Moler have observed that Darcy is set up to be deflated, that he is in fact a caricature of the Burney-Richardson hero, but the character of Darcy also reflects a larger tendency in the novel to set up and subvert male power in general. See Bradbrook, *Jane Austen and Her Predecessors*, p. 97; Moler, *Jane Austen's Art of Allusion*, p. 89.
8. See Nina Auerbach's fine chapter on *Pride and Prejudice*: "The unexpressed intensity of this collective waiting for the door to open and a Pygmalion to bring life into limbo defines the female world of *Pride and Prejudice*." *Communities of Women*, p. 39.
9. Though see Auerbach on the way in which the Bennet women's economic invisibility is subtly expressed in the "near invisibility of Longbourn and the collective life of the Bennets within." Ibid., p. 42.
10. It is hardly surprising that readers of *Pride and Prejudice* are widely divergent in their assessment of the Charlotte Lucas episode. A few, for example, sympathize with Charlotte and see her, more or less, as a victim of economic and social necessity. See David Daiches, "Jane Austen, Karl Marx, and the Aristocratic Dance," *American Scholar* 17 (1947–1948): 289; and see

Mark Schorer, "Pride Unprejudiced," *Kenyon Review* 18 (1956): 83, 85. On the other end of the spectrum, many critics are inclined to see Charlotte as a rather simple example of moral or intellectual perversity. See W. A. Craik, *Jane Austen*, p. 65, and Jane Nardin, *Those Elegant Decorums*, p. 51.

11. Several critics observe elements, at least, of wish fulfillment or self-projection in Austen's heroines. See, for example, Yasmine Gooneratne, *Jane Austen*, p. 95.
12. Hobsbawm, *Age of Revolution*, p. 218.
13. John B. Owen, *The Eighteenth Century*, p. 314.
14. Watt, *Rise of the Novel*, p. 61.
15. See Auerbach on the safety of being "partial, prejudiced, and ignorant. Objectivity, impartiality, and knowledge might endanger the cloak of invisibility which is so intrinsic a part of Austen's perception of a woman's life." *Communities of Women*, p. 54.
16. See Auerbach's description of Pemberley's "architectural and natural power." Ibid., p. 44.
17. While it is true, as Gilbert and Gubar maintain, that Austen's stories dramatize "the necessity of female submission for female survival," the end of *Pride and Prejudice* is managed so as to mitigate the degree to which the heroine must submit. *Madwoman in the Attic*, p. 154.
18. Several critics note that Darcy is more convincing as villain than as hero. See, for example, Henrietta Ten Harmsel, *Jane Austen*, p. 81. And Kenneth Moler, for one, finds Elizabeth becoming more and more like the conventional Evelina; see *Austen's Art of Allusion*, p. 107. See also Nina Auerbach's treatment of Darcy's "shadowy reality," in *Communities of Women*, p. 53.

3. *Villette*

1. Austen, *Pride and Prejudice*, p. 229.
2. Charlotte Brontë, *Villette*, ed. Geoffrey Tillotson and Donald Hawes, p. 5. Subsequent references appear in the text.
3. Andrew Hook, "Charlotte Brontë, The Imagination, and *Villete*," in *The Brontës*, ed. Ian Gregor, p. 145.
4. I differ here from Helene Moglen, who finds the Bretton household "a household warmed by love" and who attributes the focus on Polly, along with Lucy's distance from Polly's experi-

ence, to Lucy's inability to recognize in herself "an overwhelming need and capacity for love." See *Charlotte Brontë*, pp. 199, 200.

5. *Villette*, in contrast to *Jane Eyre*, is not a novel that gives emphasis to the richness of relations between women. In every relation between Lucy and another woman in this novel, the other woman is preoccupied with a man and, what is more, without men the confined spaces of leisured female existence are made to seem cut off from life and even unhealthy. In the Miss Marchmont episode, especially, women's world shrinks to "two hot, close rooms," a narrowness which goes a long way toward making an emotional invalid of Lucy: "I forgot that there were fields, woods, rivers, seas, an ever-changing sky outside the steam-dimmed lattice of this sick-chamber; I was almost content to forget it. All within me became narrowed to my lot" (31, 32).
6. According to Harold Perkin, "entrepreneurial class society . . . was based on the moral conception of work," and it was by persuading the rest of society to accept this ideal, along with the primacy of capital and competition, that the capitalist middle class was able to achieve its aims. See *The Origins of Modern English Society*, pp. 277, 272.
7. Feminists like Josephine Butler, Bessie Parks, and Frances Cobbe continued to endorse the notion that "the immense majority of women are, and ought to be, employed in the noble duties which go to make up the Christian household." See Bessie Rayner Parks, *Essays on Woman's Work*, p. 222. But they argued the necessity of opening traditionally masculine occupations to single women and they endorsed the respectability of the working life: "Idleness, which is the root of all evil for men, is not particularly suited to be the root of all virtue for women. In truth, every woman of sense knows that it is precisely the want of suitable and hopeful work which is the great bane and peril of her sex. . . . women who support themselves successfully, or aid their husbands by real work at home, are the happiest and most morally safe of their sex." See Cobbe, "The Final Cause of Woman," pp. 20–21.
8. According to Terry Eagleton, the Brontës felt both "the simple imperative to earn a living—the need for energy and drive, the respect for whatever was hardy, shrewd and stoical" and "fascination with the genteel coupled with a distaste for the brash and pushing." See *Myths of Power*, p. 13.

9. Charlotte Brontë, letter to Miss Wooler, 1846, quoted in Ingastina Ewbank, *Their Proper Sphere*, p. 157.
10. Charlotte Brontë, letter to Emily Brontë, June 8, 1939, quoted in Winifred Gerin, *Charlotte Brontë*, p. 144.
11. Quoted in ibid.
12. Eagleton, for example, notes Lucy's "ambiguous approval and resentment of those more successful than herself." *Myths of Power*, p. 70.
13. Ellis, *Women of England*, p. 24.
14. Moglen says: "Already plagued by the survivor's sense of inadequacy and guilt, Charlotte must easily have fallen prey to masochistic submission. She would have embraced the domination of her father and brother, accepted the social pressures as interpreted by her aunt." Later, with Monsieur Héger, she is "powerless: enslaved not by Héger but by herself: by her obsession, her need." *Charlotte Brontë*, pp. 41, 73.
15. Helene Moglen sees this as the dominant conflict in Brontë's works and life: "In [*Villette*], as in her three earlier books, it is Brontë who must try to reconcile the heroine's independent self-realization with her need to be submerged in the powerful, masculine 'other.' For Brontë it had always been impossible to accommodate these two commanding impulses which psychosexual conditioning and social reality place in extreme conflict." Ibid., p. 225.
16. It is interesting to note how much more difficult it is for Lucy to enter this world than it is for her predecessor, William Crimsworth, in *The Professor*. Crimsworth journeys to Belgium with a letter of introduction, and, although he too arrives at night, there are no incidents. He alights from his diligence, is immediately directed to an inn, arrives there in a fiacre, eats supper, and goes to bed. The next morning he sallies out into a fine day and presents his letter to a Mr. B. Mr. B. promptly assures him of a post as professor of English and Latin. What could be simpler? For Lucy Snowe, however, the world of work is far more foreign. She too arrives at night, but she loses her portmanteau, has no notion of where to put up, is given directions but is harassed by strange men, loses her way, lands at the pensionnat entirely by accident, and is hired, in the middle of the night, purely on a whim. In Lucy's case getting a job is both remarkable and haphazard. There are no letters of introduction and no network of old girls, and the job itself is not the classy position of professor but the low-paid, almost

menial, position of children's governess and maid. But what is most striking about all this is that the adventure, daring, and risk which mark Lucy's passage land her where they do—in another interior, foreign but finally familiar. A gentlewoman's place in a man's world is not to be where the action is—on the streets of London or Villette—but to be in relative seclusion, to inhabit an interior which is really an extension of the home, a "demi-convent, secluded in the built-up core of a capital" (84).

17. Nina Auerbach and Sandra Gilbert and Susan Gubar make similar points about Lucy's allegiance or identification with Beck. See Auerbach, *Communities of Women*, p. 103, and Gubar and Gilbert, *Madwoman in the Attic*, p. 408.
18. See Auerbach on the increasing unreality of Beck's power. *Communities of Women*, p. 107.
19. Kate Millett, *Sexual Politics*, p. 145.
20. See Gilbert and Gubar on Lucy's attraction to Ginevra's self-indulgence and freedom. *Madwoman in the Attic*, p. 409.
21. Moglen explains this regression psychoanalytically: "Lucy can be moved into the future only through the medium of the past. Lucy awakens to the beginning . . . the house at Bretton. We discover how deeply she cared for Graham, how Paulina had been her surrogate." *Charlotte Brontë*, p. 210.
22. Eagleton observes that "Lucy's bitterness at John's breezy treatment of her is clearly a class-issue," but he fails to note the sexual power relations for which the class issue is really a displacement. *Myths of Power*, p. 71.
23. Carol Ohmann, "Historical Reality and 'Divine Appointment' in Charlotte Brontë's Fiction," *Signs* 2 (Summer 1977): 767.
24. As Ohmann rightly notes, the conflict between a man who would dominate and a woman who'd rather he didn't is resolved with relative ease because of the terms in which Brontë poses their opposition: ". . . Brontë has Paul and Lucy collide not primarily as patriarchal man and subordinate woman . . . but as *Continental* man and *English* woman." She also notes the essential likeness of the two: "Although [Paul] is freer by far and better circumstanced than Lucy is, Paul nonetheless suffers her essential experience of deprivation." Ibid., p. 772.
25. Moglen suggests that the villainy of Silas and Walravens is an expression of Lucy's irrational fears, but it is clear, I think, that they also function as part of Brontë's attempt to reconcile her own conflicts about the independence of her heroine; *Charlotte Brontë*, p. 221. Auerbach sees Walravens as an expression of fe-

male power, "a preternatural female ruler"; *Communities of Women*, p. 107. Gilbert and Gubar see her as an image of Lucy's repressed anger; *Madwoman in the Attic*, p. 431.

26. I agree with Patricia Spacks that Lucy does not choose freedom over love, as Kate Millett suggests. She, and Brontë with her, attempt to choose both. See *Female Imagination*, p. 38. Nina Auerbach suggests that Lucy lives in a female community at the end and that the community is translated "into a seal of her triumph"; *Communities of Women*, p. 113. My own reading is closer to Gilbert and Gubar's, who suggest that Brontë wishes to have an integrated sense of self, economic independence, and male affection for her heroine but who also suggest that Brontë leaves the conclusion open-ended and elusive, "refraining from any deliberate message except to remind us of the continuing need for sustaining stories of survival"; *Madwoman in the Attic*, p. 438.

4. *The Mill on the Floss*

1. George Eliot, *The Mill on the Floss*, ed. Gordon S. Haight, p. 7. Subsequent references appear in the text.
2. As Uli C. Knoepflmacher points out, "the river becomes a metaphor for the sweeping progress of history . . ." See *George Eliot's Early Novels*, p. 180.
3. Walter Allen notes rightly that "George Eliot has never been praised enough for her grasp of the property basis of the society which she describes in *The Mill on the Floss*." See *George Eliot*, p. 122.
4. It is not quite accurate to say that "lacking masculine money, no feminine accomplishment has value," for Jane Glegg, and to a lesser degree Sophy Pullet and Bessy Tulliver, attach significance to their household arts. See Spacks, *Female Imagination*, p. 46.
5. Hobsbawm, *Age of Revolution*, pp. 335, 342.
6. Ibid., p. 335.
7. As Patricia Spacks notes, "Maggie lives in a world that provides no female models." *Female Imagination*, p. 49.
8. Eagleton, *Criticism and Ideology*, p. 111.
9. Ruby V. Redinger, *George Eliot*, p. 42.
10. Ibid., pp. 42, 92, 304, 385.
11. Laura Comer Emery, in her very helpful study of George Eliot, points out that Maggie also strikes out, unintentionally, at

Tom: "The offense itself is one outlet for Maggie's unconscious rage, and the highly emotional condemnation of Tom's severity is another." See *George Eliot's Creative Conflict*, p. 25. Nina Auerbach suggests a similar point when she draws attention to Maggie's turbulent hair as "an emblem of destructive powers she is only half aware of and unable to control." See "The Power of Hunger: Demonism and Maggie Tulliver," *Nineteenth Century Fiction* 30 (September 1975): 156.

12. Barbara Hardy also observes that Eliot "creates a pattern of apparent *Bildung*, but undermines and flattens its gains and crises." See *Critical Essays on George Eliot*, ed. Barbara Hardy, p. 53.
13. Hardy, for one, does observe that Maggie's world with Philip is "the adult equivalent of her old dreamworlds"; ibid., p. 54. But it should be noted that Maggie's childhood dreamworlds are very often fantasies of power—her world with Philip is one in which she is dependent.
14. Michael Steig also suggests that "it is plausible that Maggie's general sense of powerlessness and her exhaustion from her unavailing struggle to achieve autonomy and identity are what make her feel such a charm in submitting to Stephen." See "Anality in *The Mill on the Floss*," *Novel* 5 (Fall 1971): 52.
15. While I agree with Emery that Stephen takes the place of Tom and that he is someone with whom Maggie longs to merge or to identify, I do not feel that Maggie's relation with Tom is marked by the same longing to be passively taken care of. Tom does bait Maggie's hook when they go fishing, but this is a stage in life at which she is also bent on being clever and admired.
16. As Knoepflmacher observes, Maggie is rather suddenly transformed into a princess, "and we are not allowed to forget the 'jet crown' upon this exquisite creature's head." *George Eliot's Early Novels*, p. 207.
17. Patricia Spacks observes that "unlike Charlotte Brontë's heroines, Maggie does not long for a career"; *Female Imagination*, p. 52. But that is because George Eliot does not permit her to. It does seem, as Uli Knoepflmacher has observed, that Eliot "comes close to pretending that Maggie's destiny is absolutely sealed because sealed by 'the irreversible laws within and without her'"; *George Eliot's Early Novels*, p. 212.
18. Emery traces a similar shift in Maggie, although she explains it psychoanalytically: "The narrator guides us toward identifying

with Maggie, whose intense 'wants,' continually conflicting with hard reality, touch the inevitably frustrated infantile desires shared by all readers. . . . After Mr. Tulliver's 'downfall,' the easy balance of the first two books is replaced by extreme tension as the conflict between desire and the real world becomes an inner conflict between wants and shoulds, id and superego." See *George Eliot's Creative Conflict*, p. 33. My own reading locates the tension in Eliot's ambivalence toward the desire for power in a heroine who is now old enough to be held responsible for her own longings.

19. Knoepflmacher, *George Eliot's Early Novels*, p. 207.
20. I differ here from Emery, who sees the "crude moral judgments" made by the "world's wife" as providing a context in which "Maggie's 'act of penitence' will inevitably take on heroic proportions and thus escape undue scrutiny"; *George Eliot's Creative Conflict*, p. 51. This may indeed be one function of the narrator's blast at Maggie's community, but the narrator's unusual anger is also an expression of Eliot's own ambivalent feelings toward the fate which she has engineered for her heroine.
21. Gilbert and Gubar agree but do not locate Eliot's conservatism in her adherence to a more general ideology: "It is . . . a compensatory and conservative aspect of Eliot's fiction that associates women with precisely the traits she felt industrial urbanized England in danger of losing: a commitment to others, a sense of community, an appreciation of nature, and a belief in nurturing love." *Madwoman in the Attic*, p. 499.
22. Steig observes that "the fantasy of a golden childhood is an attempt to evade the insight that the perfect ego-ideal of Maggie's society as embodied in Tom, is incompatible with strong human sympathies"; "Anality in *The Mill on the Floss*," p. 50. This kind of fantasy is required, of course, if one is to endorse love and sacrifice for men as a woman's duty.
23. Emery, *George Eliot's Creative Conflict*, p. 24.
24. Gilbert and Gubar make a similar point: Eliot "simultaneously demonstrates the necessity of renouncing anger and the absolute impossibility of genuinely doing so"; "Eliot balances the narrator's reverence for gentle heroines with the author's vengeful impulses throughout her later fiction." *Madwoman in the Attic*, pp. 513, 499.
25. Georg Lukács, *Realism in Our Time*, p. 61.
26. Ibid.
27. Williams, *Marxism and Literature*, p. 114.

Afterword

1. The same ideological tension explains what Gilbert and Gubar have noted as a paradox in the works of female writers at midcentury: "Paradoxically, by the middle of the nineteenth century, when women were widening their political, social and educational spheres of influence and activity, women writers, in retreat from revolt, became concerned with the issue of internalization." *Madwoman in the Attic*, p. 444.
2. Parks, *Essays on Woman's Work*, p. 16; Butler, *Woman's Work and Woman's Culture*, p. xxvii; Frances Power Cobbe, *The Duties of Women*, p. 24.
3. Gilbert and Gubar, *Madwoman in the Attic*, pp. 371, 369; Eagleton, *Criticism and Ideology*, p. 97.
4. Cott, *Bonds of Womanhood*, pp. 202, 203, 205, 197, 200.
5. Elizabeth Gaskell, letter to Eliza Fox [ca. February 1850], letter 68; letter to Eliza Fox [April? 1850], letter 69; letter to Eliza Fox, December 24 [25?], 1854, letter 222. *Letters*, pp. 106, 107, 109, 325.
6. Elizabeth Gaskell, *North and South*, p. 2.
7. Quoted in Winifred Gerin, *Elizabeth Gaskell*, p. 262.
8. Showalter, *Literature of Their Own*, p. 15.

Bibliography

"Advice to Young Ladies on the Improvement of the Mind." *Edinburgh Review* 15 (January 1810): 299–315.

Allen, Walter. *George Eliot.* New York: Macmillan, 1964.

Auerbach, Nina. *Communities of Women: An Idea in Fiction.* Cambridge, Mass.: Harvard University Press, 1978.

———. "The Power of Hunger: Demonism and Maggie Tulliver." *Nineteenth Century Fiction* 30 (September 1975): 150–171.

Austen, Jane. *Jane Austen's Letters to Her Sister Cassandra and Others.* Ed. R. W. Chapman. London: Oxford University Press, 1959.

———. *Pride and Prejudice.* New York: Holt, Rinehart & Winston, 1949.

Basch, Françoise. *Relative Creatures: Victorian Women in Society and the Novel.* New York: Schocken Books, 1974.

Bradbrook, Frank W. *Jane Austen and Her Predecessors.* Cambridge, Eng.: Cambridge University Press, 1966.

Branca, Patricia. *Silent Sisterhood: Middle Class Women in the Victorian Home.* Pittsburgh: Carnegie-Mellon University Press, 1975.

Bridenthal, Renate, and Claudia Koonz, eds. *Becoming Visible: Women in European History.* Boston: Houghton Mifflin, 1977.

Brontë, Charlotte. *Villette.* Ed. Geoffrey Tillotson and Donald Hawes. Boston: Houghton Mifflin, 1971.

Buckle, Henry Thomas. "The Influence of Women on the Progress of Knowledge." *Fraser's Magazine* 57 (April 1858): 395–407.

Burney, Frances. *The Early Diary of Frances Burney, 1768–1778.* Ed. Annie Raine Ellis. 2 vols. London: George Bell & Sons, 1907.

———. *Evelina: or, The History of a Young Lady's Entrance into the World.* New York: W. W. Norton, 1965.

———. *The Journals and Letters of Fanny Burney.* Ed. Joyce Hemlow. Oxford: Clarendon Press, 1973.

Bush, Douglas. *Jane Austen.* New York: Macmillan, 1975.

Butler, Josephine E., ed. *Woman's Work and Woman's Culture: A Series of Essays*. London: Macmillan, 1869.

Carroll, Berenice A. "Peace Research: The Cult of Power." *Journal of Conflict Resolution* 16 (December 1972): 505–616.

Clark, Alice. *The Working Life of Women in the Seventeenth Century*. London: Frank Cass, 1968.

Cobbe, Frances Power. *The Duties of Women: A Course of Lectures*. Boston: Geo. H. Ellis, 1882.

———. "The Final Cause of Woman." In *Woman's Work and Woman's Culture: A Series of Essays*, ed. Josephine E. Butler, pp. 1–25. London: Macmillan, 1869.

Cott, Nancy F. *The Bonds of Womanhood: "Woman's Sphere" in New England, 1780–1835*. New Haven: Yale University Press, 1977.

Craik, W. A. *Jane Austen: The Six Novels*. London: Methuen, 1965.

Daiches, David. "Jane Austen, Karl Marx, and the Aristocratic Dance." *American Scholar* 17 (1947–1948): 289–296.

Davis, Natalie Zemon. "'Women's History' in Transition: The European Case." *Feminist Studies* 3 (Spring–Summer 1976): 83–103.

DuBois, Ellen, Mari Jo Buhle, Temma Kaplan, Gerda Lerner, and Carroll Smith-Rosenberg. "Politics and Culture in Women's History: A Symposium." *Feminist Studies* 6 (Spring 1980): 26–64.

Eagleton, Terry. *Criticism and Ideology: A Study in Marxist Literary Theory*. London: NLB, 1976.

———. "Ideology, Fiction, Narrative." *Social Text* 2 (Summer 1979): 62–80.

———. *Marxism and Literary Criticism*. Berkeley & Los Angeles: University of California Press, 1976.

———. *Myths of Power: A Marxist Study of the Brontës*. New York: Barnes & Noble, 1975.

Eliot, George. *Middlemarch*. Ed. Gordon S. Haight. Boston: Houghton Mifflin, 1956.

———. *The Mill on the Floss*. Ed. Gordon S. Haight. Boston: Houghton Mifflin, 1961.

Ellis, Sarah. *The Daughters of England: Their Position in Society, Character, and Responsibilities*, 1845; *The Wives of England: Their Relative Duties, Domestic Influence, and Social Obligations*, 1843; *The Women of England: Their Social Duties, and Domestic Habits*, 1839; rpt. in *The Family Monitor and Domestic Guide*. New York: E. Walker, n.d.

Emery, Laura Comer. *George Eliot's Creative Conflict: The Other Side of Silence*. Berkeley & Los Angeles: University of California Press, 1976.

Ewbank, Inga-Stina. *Their Proper Sphere: A Study of the Brontë Sisters as Early-Victorian Novelists*. London: Edward Arnold, 1966.

"The Female Character." *Fraser's Magazine* 7 (1833): 591–601.

"Female Labour." *Fraser's Magazine* 61 (March 1860): 359–371.

Fetterley, Judith. *The Resisting Reader*. Bloomington: Indiana University Press, 1977.

Fordyce, James. *Sermons to Young Women*. 2 vols. London: A. Millar, W. Law, & R. Cater, 1794.

Foster, Leonard. *The Icy Fire: Five Studies in European Petrarchanism*. Cambridge, Eng.: Cambridge University Press, 1969.

Foucault, Michel. "Truth and Power." In *Power/Knowledge: Selected Interviews and Other Writings, 1972–1977*, ed. Colin Gordon. New York: Pantheon Books, 1980.

Gaskell, Elizabeth. *The Letters of Mrs. Gaskell*. Ed. J. A. V. Chapple and Arthur Pollard. Cambridge, Mass.: Harvard University Press, 1967.

———. *North and South*. London: Dent, 1975.

George, Margaret. "From 'Goodwife' to 'Mistress': The Transformation of the Female in Bourgeois Culture." *Science and Society* 37 (1973): 152–177.

Gerin, Winifred. *Charlotte Brontë: The Evolution of Genius*. London: Oxford University Press, 1967.

———. *Elizabeth Gaskell: A Biography*. Oxford: Clarendon Press, 1976.

Gilbert, Sandra, and Susan Gubar. *The Madwoman in the Attic: The Woman Writer and the Nineteenth-Century Literary Imagination*. New Haven: Yale University Press, 1979.

Gisborne, Thomas. *An Enquiry into the Duties of the Female Sex*. Philadelphia: James Humphreys, 1798.

Gooneratne, Yasmine. *Jane Austen*. Cambridge, Eng.: Cambridge University Press, 1970.

Gordon, Ann D., Mari Jo Buhle, and Nancy Schrom Dye. "The Problem of Women's History." In *Liberating Women's History: Theoretical and Critical Essays*, ed. Berenice A. Carroll, pp. 75–92. Urbana: University of Illinois Press, 1976.

Gordon, Linda, and Allen Hunter. "Sex, Family, and the New Right: Anti-Feminism as a Political Force." *Radical America* 11 (Winter 1977–1978): 9–25.

Gregor, Ian, ed. *The Brontës: A Collection of Critical Essays*. Englewood Cliffs, N.J.: Prentice-Hall, 1970.

Gregory, John. *A Father's Legacy to His Daughters*. New York: Garland Publishing, 1974.

Haber, Barbara. "Is Personal Life Still a Political Issue?" *Feminist Studies* 5 (Fall 1979): 417–430.

Hardy, Barbara, ed. *Critical Essays on George Eliot*. London: Routledge & Kegan Paul, 1970.

Hartmann, Heidi. "Capitalism, Patriarchy, and Job Segregation by Sex." *Signs* 1 (1976): 137–169.

Hemlow, Joyce. *The History of Fanny Burney*. Oxford: Clarendon Press, 1958.

Hiller, Dana V., and Robin Ann Sheets, eds. *Women and Men: The Consequences of Power: A Collection of New Essays*. Cincinnati: Office of Women's Studies, University of Cincinnati, 1977.

Hobsbawm, Eric J. *The Age of Revoluton: 1789–1848*. New York: New American Library, 1962.

———. *Industry and Empire*. Vol. 3 of *The Pelican Economic History of Britain*. Baltimore: Penguin Books, 1968.

Holcombe, Lee. *Victorian Ladies at Work: Middle-Class Working Women in England and Wales, 1850–1914*. Newton Abbot: David & Charles, 1973.

Houghton, Walter E. *The Victorian Frame of Mind, 1830–1870*. New Haven: Yale University Press, 1957.

Howe, Florence. "Women and the Power to Change." In *Women and the Power to Change*, ed. Florence Howe, pp. 127–169. New York: McGraw-Hill, 1975.

Jameson, Fredric. *Marxism and Form: Twentieth-Century Dialectical Theories of Literature*. Princeton: Princeton University Press, 1971.

———. *The Political Unconscious: Narrative as a Socially Symbolic Act*. Ithaca, N.Y.: Cornell University Press, 1981.

Janeway, Elizabeth. "On the Power of the Weak." *Signs* 1 (1975): 103–109.

Johansson, Sheila Ryan. "'Herstory' as History: A New Field or Another Fad?" In *Liberating Women's History: Theoretical and Critical Essays*, ed. Berenice A. Carroll, pp. 400–430. Urbana: University of Illinois Press, 1976.

Kennard, Jean E. *Victims of Convention*. Hamden, Conn.: Archon Books, 1978.

Kinnear, John Boyd. "The Social Position of Women in the Present

Age." In *Woman's Work and Woman's Culture: A Series of Essays*, ed. Josephine E. Butler, pp. 332–366. London: Macmillan, 1869.

Knoepflmacher, Uli C. *George Eliot's Early Novels: The Limits of Realism*. Berkeley & Los Angeles: University of California Press, 1968.

Laslett, Peter. *The World We Have Lost*. New York: Charles Scribner's Sons, 1965.

Legates, Marlene. "The Cult of Womanhood in Eighteenth-Century Thought." *Eighteenth-Century Studies* 10 (Fall 1976): 21–39.

Lerner, Gerda. "Placing Women in History: A 1975 Perspective." In *Liberating Women's History: Theoretical and Critical Essays*, ed. Berenice A. Carroll, pp. 357–367. Urbana: University of Illinois Press, 1976.

Lewis, C. S. *The Allegory of Love: A Study in Medieval Tradition*. New York: Oxford University Press, 1958.

Lougee, Carolyn C. "Modern European History." *Signs* 2 (1977): 628–650.

Lukács, Georg. *Realism in Our Time: Literature and the Class Struggle*. New York: Harper & Row, 1964.

Macherey, Pierre. *A Theory of Literary Production*. Trans. Geoffrey Wall. London: Routledge & Kegan Paul, 1978.

Millett, Kate. *Sexual Politics*. Garden City, N.Y.: Doubleday, 1970.

Moers, Ellen. *Literary Women*. Garden City, N.Y.: Doubleday, 1976.

Moglen, Helene. *Charlotte Brontë: The Self Conceived*. New York: Norton, 1976.

Moler, Kenneth. *Jane Austen's Art of Allusion*. Lincoln: University of Nebraska Press, 1968.

Newton, Judith Lowder. "*Evelina*: or, The History of a Young Lady's Entrance into the Marriage Market." *Modern Language Studies* 6 (Spring 1976): 27–42.

Ohmann, Carol. "Historical Reality and 'Divine Appointment' in Charlotte Brontë's Fiction." *Signs* 2 (Summer 1977): 757–778.

Owen, John B. *The Eighteenth Century: 1714–1815*. Totowa, N.J.: Rowman & Littlefield, 1962.

Parks, Bessie Rayner. *Essays on Woman's Work*. 2d ed. London: Alexander Strahan, 1865.

Perkin, Harold. *The Origins of Modern English Society: 1780–1880*. London: Routledge & Kegan Paul, 1969.

Pinchbeck, Ivy. *Women Workers and the Industrial Revolution: 1750–1850*. New York: Augustus M. Kelley, 1969.

P.M.Y. "Woman and Her Social Position." *Westminster Review* 35 (January 1841): 13–27.

Redinger, Ruby V. *George Eliot: The Emergent Self*. New York: Alfred A. Knopf, 1975.

Richards, Eric. "Women in the British Economy since about 1700: An Interpretation." *History* 59 (October 1974): 337–357.

Richetti, John J. *Popular Fiction before Richardson: Narrative Patterns 1700–1739*. Oxford: Clarendon Press, 1969.

"Rights and Conditions of Women." *Edinburgh Review* 73 (January 1841): 189–209.

Robinson, Lillian S. *Sex, Class, and Culture*. Bloomington: Indiana University Press, 1978.

Rosaldo, Michelle Zimbalist, and Louise Lamphere, eds. *Woman, Culture, and Society*. Stanford: Stanford University Press, 1974.

Rosenberg, Charles E. *The Family in History*. Philadelphia: University of Pennsylvania Press, 1975.

Schorer, Mark. "Pride Unprejudiced." *Kenyon Review* 18 (1956): 72–91.

Selsam, Howard, David Goldway, and Harry Martel, eds. *Dynamics of Social Change: A Reader in Marxist Social Science*. New York: International Publishers, 1970.

Showalter, Elaine. *A Literature of Their Own: British Women Novelists from Brontë to Lessing*. Princeton: Princeton University Press, 1977.

Spacks, Patricia. *The Female Imagination*. New York: Avon Books, 1972.

"Spirit of Society in England and France." *Edinburgh Review* 52 (January 1831): 374–387.

Stage, Sarah. "Women's History and 'Woman's Sphere': Major Works of the 1970s." *Socialist Review* 50/51 (March–June 1980): 245–253.

Steeves, Harrison R. *Before Jane Austen: The Shaping of the English Novel in the Eighteenth Century*. New York: Holt, Rinehart & Winston, 1965.

Steig, Michael. "Anality in *The Mill on the Floss*." *Novel* 5 (Fall 1971): 42–53.

Ten Harmsel, Henrietta. *Jane Austen: A Study in Fictional Conventions*. London: Mouton, 1964.

Utter, Robert Palfrey, and Gwendolyn Bridges Needham. *Pamela's Daughters*. New York: Macmillan, 1936.

Vogel, Lise. "The Contested Domain: A Note on the Family in the

Transition to Capitalism." *Marxist Perspectives* 1 (Spring 1978): 50–73.

Watson, Barbara Bellow. "On Power and the Literary Text." *Signs* 1 (1975): 111–118.

Watt, Ian. *The Rise of the Novel*. Berkeley & Los Angeles: University of California Press, 1962.

Williams, Raymond. *Marxism and Literature*. Oxford: Oxford University Press, 1977.

Index